how2become

A Mobile Hairdresser The Insider's Guide

Katie Morris

D1583823

Orders: Please contact How2become Ltd, Suite 2, 50 Churchill Square Business Centre, Kings Hill, Kent ME19 4YU. You can also order via the e mail address info@how2become.co.uk and at Gardners.com.

ISBN: 9781907558979

First published 2012

Typeset for How2become Ltd by Molly Hill, Canada.

Printed in Great Britain for How2become Ltd by Bell & Bain Ltd, 303 Burnfield Road, Thornliebank, Glasgow G46 7UQ.

CONTENTS

INTRODUCTION

Back in the days of Vidal Sassoon, hairdressing was under-stood to be a precision skill, practiced by many, mastered by few. In later years, thanks in part to relatively low wages, hairdressing developed a reputation as a 'second class' career – when nothing could have been further from the truth.

Today, hairdressing is a vibrant and thriving industry, with the rise of the celebrity hairdresser bringing back into the lime-light one of the most important elements of style.

How important is a good hairstyle? Watch any makeover programme on TV: It doesn't matter how much surgery, den-tal treatment, make-up or expensive clothes a person is given. It is only when the stylist gets his hands on their hair that the true transformation takes place. The vast majority of us notice other people's hair before we notice anything else!

A career as a hairdresser today can take you down many roads, from working in a salon to TV celebrity, from free-lancing to stage and film. Many hairdressers spend their whole careers servicing the needs of a small section of the

community - working in a barbers, for example, or visiting old folks' homes. Others build up a dedicated following of clients who wouldn't trust another living soul with their precious hair. A few rise all the way to the top, winning competitions, styling the stars, developing brands along the way.

None of these careers is any more or less important or impressive than the other – each have their place in the hairdressing world, and the industry is better for the variety they bring.

This book is aimed at anyone interested in branching out into the world of mobile hairdressing. Mobile hairdressing is defined here as a professional, qualified hairdresser visiting clients in their homes or places of work to offer hairdressing services. Far from a soft-option, mobile hairdressing is both tough and rewarding – a viable alternative to opening a salon in times of high rental values on commercial premises and ever-increasing costs.

HOW TO USE THIS BOOK

Mobile Hairdressing Explained is organised into six chapters covering everything you need to know to become a successful business owner and to take your business forward. The chapters follow a logical pattern and, if you have the time, the best way to read this book is from start to finish. However, I know that some of you will want to skip to the bit that is most relevant, or seems the most interesting, and dip in and out in whatever order suits. This is fine, and in the next section I have provided a brief summary of each chapter. This will also provide a handy reference point later should you wish to revisit a particular area or topic.

If you are currently working as a mobile hairdresser but are

struggling with losing clients, you may want to take a look at Chapter Four: Your Most Important Asset: Clients, and then move on to Chapter Six: Growing Your Business. If you are getting bogged down with paperwork, skip to Chapter Five for advice on everything financial.

You may, however, be simply weighing up your options and considering mobile hairdressing alongside other career choices. This is a great resource for helping you make that important decision and I would recommend you start with Chapter One: Reasons for Starting Your Own Business, and then skip to the last chapter to see where your career could take you.

CHAPTER SUMMARIES

Chapter One: Reasons for Starting Your Own Business
Assess your own motivations and capabilities and discover whether self-employment is for you. Explore the upside and the downside to running your own business before taking the plunge.

Chapter Two: Getting Started
Understand the tax and legal implications of being self-employed and learn all about planning. Who is your competition? What will your business be called? Answer all these questions and produce a business plan you can use to guide you – or to gain valuable investment.

Chapter Three: Building Your Business
Use every tool available to you to build up your business base. Advertising, referrals, leaflets, discounts, posters and special offers – learn how to use these to pull in clients from many sources. Consider building a website and keep an eye on which form of advertising works best.

Chapter Four: Your Most Important Asset: Clients
Always keep an eye on keeping your clients happy. Explore

the reasons why hairdressers lose clients and learn how to avoid common pitfalls. Become a expert in customer care with questionnaires, newsletters and follow-up services. Be prepared for difficult situations and learn how to deal with them calmly and confidently.

Chapter Five: Financial Matters
Explore all things financial – without fear! Learn how to keep records, manage your banking and produce accounts. With sample forms and spreadsheets to get your business up and running in no time.

Chapter Six: Growing Your Business
Don't get stale! Prepare now for keeping on top of your business growth with ideas for increasing your revenue without increasing your effort. Learn how to recognise, and capitalise on, your 'A' clients. And keep your skills current and on trend with training and investing in yourself.

CHAPTER I

REASONS FOR STARTING YOUR OWN BUSINESS

Working for yourself. What an amazing dream. But it doesn't have to remain a dream: millions of people run their own businesses, people just like you. This may surprise you but hairdressers are especially suited to working for themselves. Your typical hairdresser is confident and outgoing; essential qualities for building up a client base or going to ask your bank manager for a loan, and hairdressers are great at multi-tasking; a bonus when you have to be receptionist, accountant, promoter and sales person all rolled into one!

Hairdressers have fantastic time-management skills (that's what it's called when you get through a day with a double column and nobody turns up on time), are hardworking, determined, and creative. All these qualities are the bedrock of entrepreneurs and all you need is the knowledge of how to put them into practise.

So why work for yourself? Isn't it easier just to go to work and come home without any worry or responsibility? To have

the security of regular wages, holiday pay and sick pay?

OF COURSE IT IS! But just because it's easier, doesn't mean it's better. What about freedom, to choose the hours you work and the type of clients you see? What about the potential to have no limits on your earnings and to keep all the profits for yourself?

And what about the satisfaction of knowing that YOU did it? You built your business up from nothing and look at you now!

> ***Consider this:*** Being self employed isn't for everyone and there is nothing wrong with valuing the regular and the secure. Some types of job simply don't lend themselves to working alone – it would be difficult for a policeman or a nurse to be self-employed. But if the idea of setting up your own business lights a fire inside you then you owe it to yourself to give it a go.

FINANCIAL INDEPENDENCE

One of the biggest lures for the self-employed is the idea of financial independence. What does this actually mean? There are many degrees of financial independence from having enough money in the bank to never have to work again (from a lottery win, perhaps), to being free of debt and having a regular income.

My personal definition is having enough savings to cover your outgoings for at least six months should you become ill, and having the means to earn in excess of your needs without having to strain yourself by working ridiculously long hours. And to be able to afford and enjoy all those little necessities like long holidays, good living and whatever else floats your boat.

In the planning section of this book you will have the opportunity to set your personal survival budget. This is the minimum amount you need to earn to survive, while still paying your rent or mortgage, and managing to eat. But financial independence should be about more than merely meeting these needs. It is knowing that your financial future is not dependant on another person or organisation.

Even if you have a solid job, are well thought of and a good employee, there is always the chance of redundancy. Salons close everyday – no matter how good you are at your job, the salons' owner may not be great at running a business. Management changes, personalities clash, clients come and go. The only true security comes from being in charge of your own employment – and this is the basis of self-employment.

The great news is that hairdressing is one of the skills that is widely recognised as being perfectly suited to self-employment. It is also virtually recession-proof – people will always need their hair cutting, even if they choose to cut back on colours or perms. Hair grows, no matter what a person's financial situation. So hairdressers are ideally placed to build a life and a career for themselves that is dependant only on their own skills and efforts.

Why is it then, that some mobile hairdressers do fail to make a decent living, and a few end up back in salons, working for someone else, with horror stories about where it all went wrong? The answer is simple – they didn't read this book before they started!

POSSIBLE EARNINGS

At the time of writing, a mobile hairdresser can earn anything from £5,000 a year for part-time evening work to in excess of

 how2become

£35,000 per annum. With add-on services and other expansion ideas, your earnings have no ceiling other than your own imagination and the amount of effort you are willing to put in.

Case study:
Nicola from Leeds had worked in a city centre salon for three years when she decided to become self-employed. Nicola says: 'I use to add up my takings for the week and couldn't believe my wages were such a small percentage of the amount I'd actually taken.' Nicola recognised that the salon had other overheads, such as rent and bills, but still felt she could do better by herself. Now she has been mobile for five years.

'Many of my clients came with me at first, but a lot of them liked the salon experience so they drifted away. I had to work hard to find more, but now I'm busy most days.' Nicola paid herself £22,000 last year. She also put some of her profits back into the business by buying a new car and some new equipment. 'I can't see any reason why my business shouldn't keep on growing,' says Nicola. 'Next year I predict I will earn around £28,000.'

FREEDOM

Maybe what appeals to you most isn't the potential income but the idea of being in charge of your own life – the hours you work, what time you have to get up in the morning, whether you will work weekends or not. If so, then being self employed is definitely for you. In fact, you will probably find that once you've run your own business you will be virtually unemployable! All the more incentive to make the business work...

CHOOSING YOUR OWN HOURS OF WORK

Once you have completed the planning section in Chapter Two: Getting Started, you'll know how many hours a week you need to work to survive. You'll then be able to decide for yourself when those hours should be – bearing in mind that clients have to be available at those times also! It's no good deciding you want to do all of your work at night if you want to be a mobile hairdresser.

The reality is that mobile hairdressing is most suited to people who are happy to work most evenings, and at least a couple of hours at the weekend. If you're not much of a morning person it shouldn't be too much of a problem, unless your target clients are businesses men and women who will want trims and blow-drys before they start work.

It's possible to construct your day to have a morning 'session' and an afternoon/evening session, with a few hours in between to rest and catch up on any chores or paperwork (yes, there will be paperwork). Other hairdressers work through the day, keeping office hours and finishing at six. Some prefer a more varied approach and simply work whenever their clients ask them to. Over time you will find out which approach works best for you.

Whichever hours you choose to work the important thing is to be as flexible as you can. There will always be a client who wants that little bit more – an early morning blow-dry, a Sunday afternoon trim. Choosing to be flexible is one of the bonuses of mobile hairdressing – if you worked in a salon the owner might not be happy about opening up on a Sunday for one client, or the local by-laws may not allow it.

TIP: *Flexibility is one of the many ways you can gain loyal clients who will come to see that there are many benefits to having their hair done at home.*

STATUS

Wouldn't it be great to introduce yourself to people as a business owner?

'I run my own hairdressing business,' is met with admiration and interest. (It is also a great way of getting new clients.) The status associated with running a business should not be underestimated – it sets you apart and gives you membership of an exclusive club: The club of entrepreneurs.

With this status comes responsibility, of course. The responsibility to be in charge of yourself, to make your own decisions, to complete your tax returns on time! Other business owners recognise this effort, and those who only dream of working for themselves envy it. It isn't an easy life – but it is an exciting one.

HOW MOBILE HAIRDRESSERS ARE VIEWED TODAY

There was a time when mobile hairdressers were viewed a little suspiciously. 'Are they trained properly?' people might ask, or 'Couldn't they get a job in a salon?' Thankfully, this is no longer the case. Professional organisations like the Freelance Hair and Beauty Federation have worked hard to elevate the image of mobile hairdressers to sit on an equal footing with stylists in salons.

> **Consider this:** Many mobile hairdressers have vastly more experience than salon stylists. They have often worked in different locations, built up clienteles many times over, and train constantly to keep up to date.

Another factor which has changed the public's perception of mobile hairdressing is the changes to our lifestyles, for example more and more women going back to work after

having children, and more people commuting greater distances than ever before. This has made travelling to a salon more difficult, and increased the attractiveness of having the salon come to the home.

Now, far from being treated with suspicion, good mobile hairdressers are pounced on with gratitude! Many working mothers find that being able to have the whole family's hair done at home in the evening or weekend is a huge bonus, saving both time and money. Providing the industry keeps on being supported by qualified, professional hairdressers, this profile can only get better and better.

CHALLENGE

What if going it alone fills you with fear? You are not unusual. In fact, if you didn't feel some fear about giving up the security of a regular wage and setting up alone I'd probably say you were a little crazy! In the words of the fabulous Susan Jeffers, the secret is to 'feel the fear and do it anyway'.

As hairdressers, we challenge ourselves all the time. Every time we walk up to a new client it is a challenge – a journey into the unknown. Will this person like what I do? Do I have the right skills? Will I be able to interpret their wishes? Will we have anything to talk about? (This becomes even more pronounced when it is just you and your client alone in their house!)

First and foremost you must do what you always do – trust in yourself. Be honest – if what you have read so far doesn't excite you then self-employment may not be for you. Skip to the next section; The Reality Of Working For Yourself, just to be completely sure. If what you read there really puts you off then send this book to a colleague and breathe a sigh of relief. You just had a lucky escape.

Still with us? GREAT! Then you are up for the challenge, and you will find running your own business one of the most rewarding experiences of your life.

THE EXCITEMENT OF GOING IT ALONE

Setting off on the journey of self-employment is best viewed as a big adventure. Along the way you will inevitably come up against all sorts of obstacles – money, difficult clients, lack of bookkeeping skills, time-management, and equipment breakdowns just some of them – but once you overcome these obstacles you will feel a sense of achievement like no other.

Your family might be sceptical at first, as might friends or existing clients. The more committed you are, the easier it will be to convince them you are doing the right thing. Ultimately, the only person you really need to convince is yourself. You are the only person who is living your life, and you will be the one getting up day after day working on your business and servicing your clients.

When there are decisions to be made you will have to make them yourself – and there will be no one to blame but you if the decision was the wrong one! Scary? Yes, but also exciting and invigorating. No more having to check with others before taking a step forward. No more looking for your boss's approval.

Case study:
Stephen knew within a year that he wasn't 'cut out' for working for someone else. 'I kept moving from salon to salon,' he says, 'after falling out with my manager.' Worried at first that his career as a hairdresser would be short-lived, he has found surprising success as a mobile hairdresser.

'Now I am my own boss I'm happy to work the kind of hours I would have refused to work if someone else had asked me to. I can see now I was a nightmare employee – I just hated being told what to do!'

Stephen ploughed everything into setting up his business, and being young his family were understandably worried. But he says the risk has more than paid off, and recently a client offered to back him in setting up his own salon. *'I don't think I will do it, though,'* Stephen says. *'I wouldn't want to have staff working for me if they acted the way I did!'*

EXPLORING YOUR CAPABILITIES

Before we move on to the next section, it's time to do a quick test. Don't worry, it's a test you already know the answers to – it is all about you.

Think of it like a stock-check. We need to take a look at which skills and qualities you will need to successfully run your own mobile hairdressing business (your capabilities) and then find out which of them you have already and which you will have to acquire somehow along the way.

Read through the following and place a tick next to the statements that apply to you:

1.	I am a fully qualified hairdresser	✓
2.	I have a full driving licence (and use of a car)	✓
3.	I am good at managing my time	
4.	I can motivate myself to keep going when things get tough	
5.	I am confident and outgoing, and enjoy meeting new people	

6.	People find me easy to talk to and comfortable to be around	
7.	I have good general health and am reasonably fit	
8.	I know my local area well	
9.	I am good at reading maps	
10.	I have a client base to build on	
11.	I have a supportive partner or family	
12.	I have space at home for a small office area	
13.	I'm good with numbers	
14.	I understand spreadsheets and accounts	

Now you have completed the stock-check, take a look and see what you have to work with. Numbers 1 and 2 – are pretty much essential before you can start working as a mobile hairdresser, so if you are still considering hairdressing as a career, and mobile hairdressing as the direction you wish to take, focus on these first.

Statements 3 to 6, is all about your personality and whether you have what it takes to get started. Don't worry if you can't tick all of them yet, though it is great if you can. Most hairdressers should be able to agree with statements 5 and 6, but others may need to work on their time-management and/or motivation.

The final set of statements, numbers 7 to 14, relate to more specific business skills and circumstances. It is important to be able to tick number 7, as mobile hairdressing is a physically demanding job and you won't get paid for being off sick! Knowing your local area helps, as does map-reading, but these skills can be learned.

If you have a client base to build on all the better. It isn't disloyal to your exiting salon to take your clients with you – it is the way of the industry. What counts is how you do it. On no account try to poach clients while you are working out your notice – this is both unethical and unprofessional.

If a client asks where you are moving to, you are perfectly free to tell them you are setting up alone, for example, and to ask them to look out in the local paper for your advert. When you leave your current salon, you can place an ad in the paper with a photograph for yourself and your name and contact details – existing clients are then free to get in touch along with new ones.

Your home-life matters a great deal if you are going to go into business for yourself. If you have a partner or live with family it will affect them – possibly financially, and you'll be around the house a lot more and at different times. Your life will be a lot easier if they are all on-board from the start.

TIP: *Keep your family or partner informed from day one – don't spring the idea on them after you have already given up your job. Suggest that you will give it a try for a set period, for example one year, and then look for another permanent position with a salon if it doesn't seem to be working out. And don't rely on them to bail you out if it doesn't work!*

You'll also need a small space to keep your files – customer records and information, leaflets, business cards, accounts and lots more. This could be your own office or just a corner of your bedroom; the important thing is that nobody else needs to disturb your files or use the space when you're not there.

Being good with numbers and understanding spreadsheets is something you may not be able to tick just yet, but don't

worry – after reading this book you will definitely be able to cross off the latter, and be well on your way to agreeing with the former. If you still find that numbers and accounts defeat you, simply factor into your costs a really good accountant and let them do all the work for you!

THE REALITY OF WORKING FOR YOURSELF

Which brings us to the reality of running your own business. This section is not about trying to put you off, but there are a few serious factors to consider before taking the plunge...

So far we have focused on all the positives; financial independence, freedom, status and challenge. But this wouldn't be an accurate guide to setting up a mobile hairdressing business if we didn't mention the negatives as well. There aren't many, but they are worth considering before you hand in your notice at your existing job, or start placing adverts in the local paper and ordering your business cards.

THE DOWNSIDE TO BEING SELF-EMPLOYED

Everything has a downside, and the downside to self-employment is the direct opposite to all that is great about it. For freedom, the downside is uncertainty. For flexibility, it is too much, or too little of anything. When working for yourself, you will have to work very hard initially to build up a clientele and establish your credibility. The money will roll in eventually, but to start off with it may be in short supply. If your home is your base there is no escape; from the phone, from your paperwork, from your stock and equipment.

Unless you make adequate provision, or take out an expensive insurance policy, there is no sick pay – and you will be working so hard that it is easy to get run down. Taking time

off is not only unpaid but will be met with a chorus of disapproval by your loyal, and demanding, clients.

Holidays

It is essential to plan your holidays a long way ahead, for two reasons:

1. Out of courtesy to your clients

2. So you don't miss out on any work, or end up losing clients!

You might think that taking a holiday won't make any difference to your profits – surely all your clients will fit in either before or after you go away? Yes – and no. Let's look at an example to illustrate:

Suppose you charge £20 for a cut and £40 for a colour – just to keep things simple. One of your clients has her hair done every six weeks. That is 8.6 times a year (52 weeks divided by 6). Say she has her hair coloured every second appointment, her average yearly spend would be £258 (average spend of £30 x 8.6).

If you went away twice a year, and this particular client had to push her appointment back by two or three weeks each time, her average yearly spend drops to £234 – a difference of £24. Doesn't sound a lot? This is only one client. Multiply this by only 50% of an average clientele (an average clientele would be around 60 clients), and you have a yearly loss of £720! (We said you'd be good with numbers by the end of this book!)

Remember, that is only the loss you are making on clients missing out on your services – it doesn't even take into account how you are going to cover your bills while you are away, or the cost of the holiday itself.

Now imagine if could plan things a little better and reverse the calculation. If you encouraged your clients to have their hair done before you go away, and planned it far enough in advance to fit them all in, the same numbers work out to an extra £360 over the year – something to put towards your holiday at least!

As well as the financial implications of holidays, it is also worth considering ways to keep your clients loyal to stop them simply going elsewhere while you are away. Clients can be a fickle bunch. They wake up one morning and their hair looks a bit of a mess, they see a new style on TV or on the way to work, and suddenly they have to have that hairstyle RIGHT NOW! They can't reach you. No matter – what about that other mobile hairdresser who advertises every week. Give them a try. Now you have the cost of replacing that client, with advertising, incentives and time.

All this doesn't sound too encouraging, but again, it is just another reality of being self-employed. Running your own mobile hairdressing business will require a lot more planning than merely getting up in the morning and getting yourself to work, and holidays need more thought than simply where would you like to go.

Sickness

Many self-employed people believe that they simply cannot afford to get sick. To some extent this is true – there is no sick pay for those who work for themselves. (There was a time, no so very long ago, where many salons didn't pay sick pay either, but thankfully this is changing – and there is always the measly government Statutory Sick Pay for the employed.)

The best strategy to employ is prevention – keep yourself as healthy as you can. Not too many late nights, eat well, drink

plenty of water and get plenty of fresh air and exercise. But this aside, nobody can help catching the odd bug or virus. Should you struggle on regardless, worried about paying the bills at the end of the month?

The answer is No. The last thing your clients want is their hairdresser turning up with a streaming cold, sneezing and sniffing over their heads. They may moan initially when you call to cancel but they will not thank you for passing on your germs. If you do find yourself unable to work, it is best to call all your clients immediately and let them know.

> **Consider this:** Another reality of working for yourself – when you are ill you may have to call ten to fifteen people to cancel, rather than having to make only one phone call to work when you are employed!

There is a risk that your client will go elsewhere, but it is one you will have to accept. Usually clients are happy to rebook for another day – just be sure to give yourself enough time to fully recover first, or you will have to go through the same process again!

There are insurance policies available to the self-employed which promise to pay out if your are unable to work through sickness. If you find one you like by all means go for it, but do read the small print very carefully. Many of these policies sound good in theory, but have clauses which make them virtually worthless. For example, few will pay out for the first four weeks of any illness.

A better insurance policy is to have your own savings. Financial guru, Alvin Hall, recommends having enough money saved to cover at least three months worth of outgoings – preferably six months! It may not be possible to begin your business with this security, but it is worth keeping in mind.

Ask yourself the question – what would I do if I couldn't work for any reason? Only when you know the answer, and are happy with it, should you proceed.

Loneliness
It may sound a little crazy to suggest that a hairdresser could get lonely. Aren't you out with clients all day long? Don't you have more conversations in a day than most people have in a week?

One thing you will discover very quickly when you begin working as a mobile hairdresser is that not having any colleagues to talk to can be very lonely indeed. If you work in a salon now, notice the way you talk to your co-workers, and when. Does it help to have someone's ear to bend when a client gets frustratingly difficult? Is there a particular colleague you go to when there is an issue you're not 100% sure about? What about lunchtimes and tea-breaks? Who do you talk to?

Consider this: The reality of working for yourself is that you will be working by yourself.

Yes, you will have plenty of clients to chat to. But you won't have any colleagues to share stories or tips with, to moan at or to laugh with. Unless you live close enough to your last client, lunches will probably be taken in your car with only the radio for company. If there is a problem, it is you and you alone who will have to deal with it.

Sound scary? It can be. Organisations like the Freelance Hair and Beauty Federation do offer advice and a helpline to their members, and mobile hairdressers can and do get together in local groups. But out there on the front line it will be only you, working on your own, managing on your own.

TIP: *If you are the kind of person who may find this difficult,*

consider setting up an extended support network before you start working for yourself.

Training

If you are currently working in a good salon, they probably organise regular training days so their staff can up-skill and keep their current skills up-to-date and relevant. The training may be in-house, where educators from outside companies visit the salon or one of the top stylists shares their skills, or off-site, with the staff visiting a training centre or school.

How do you feel after these training events? Fired-up? Invigorated? Eager to try your new skills on your clients?

When you are working as a mobile hairdresser, you will still need to have these regular injections of enthusiasm – as much for your benefit as for your clients. Without training, you will become stale and rusty. Your clients will notice. They will begin to drift elsewhere.

If your enthusiasm starts to go, it will become harder and harder to summon up the energy to do any work at all. Clients will fall away and you won't bother looking for more. Your list will get shorter and shorter, your earnings less and less. Eventually you will either give up hairdressing all together, believing you just don't like it anymore, or run screaming back to a salon!

Many, many mobile hairdressers give up after the first year or two, and lack of training is one of the major reasons – even if it is not the reason they cited. Training serves many purposes:

• Learning new skills

• Re-connecting you with your passion

• Meeting and sharing with other hairdressers

- Something to take back to your clients and to talk about

- Breaking the routine

- Feeling like a true professional

But isn't training expensive, I hear you ask? It doesn't have to be. There are many organisations who run group training sessions at a reasonable cost, and these costs can be off-set against your earnings (see Chapter Five: Financial Matters).

TIP: Many wholesalers, such as Sally Hair and Beauty, have training centres and regularly run courses. See Further Resources at the end of this book to find out more.

All things considered, there are certainly more positives to working for yourself than there are negatives – if you are the kind of person it appeals to, and if you do it the right way. If you are still committed to going it alone, read on to find out how to get started…

CHAPTER TWO
GETTING STARTED

BEFORE YOU START

Tax & legal implications

In the UK, every person who starts their own business has a legal requirement to let the Inland Revenue know within three months of starting – otherwise you may face a penalty. Informing the IR is easy, either go online to:

http://www.hmrc.gov.uk/selfemployed/
or telephone 0845 915 4515.

You need to do this even if you haven't yet made a profit, or if you don't actually expect to make one in the first year. You will also need to submit accounts to the Inland Revenue, although you can pay an accountant to do this for you. Unless your business is very complicated, or you are very bad with numbers, it is easy to submit your own accounts via the Inland Revenue's online self-assessment service. This is covered in more detail later in *Chapter Five: Financial Matters*.

Other legal considerations include; registering a business name and taking out Public Liability Insurance. We will look at these next.

Insurance
There are many different kinds of insurance policies a mobile hairdresser may need to have, with varying degrees of importance:

- Public Liability – essential

- Car Insurance – essential

- Health Insurance – advisable but expensive

- Equipment Insurance – advisable

- Legal Cover – advisable

Public Liability Insurance protects you against being sued by a member of the public – i.e. your clients. Seem unlikely? Suppose you were colouring a client's hair and a bit of tint splashed onto their carpet? They could claim off their home contents insurance, if they have accidental damage cover, but they could just as easily expect you to pay for a new carpet!

Or suppose you accidentally broke a priceless vase with the cord of your hairdryer? Or took all the colour out of one of their towels with perm lotion? You get the picture. Anyone who is in business and dealing with the public needs this insurance, and you can't join a professional organisation, like the Freelance Hair and Beauty Federation, without it.

Consider this: Clients can also sue for injury or emotional distress – if you nicked their ear, for example, or damaged the condition of their hair really badly. In such a case you would also need **Legal Cover** to help with the expense of being taken to court.

The fact hat you will need **Car Insurance** goes without saying. Your car, or van, will be your main expense, taking into account fuel, insurance, MOTs and servicing. But then, how would you get to your clients' homes without it? You could consider cycling, or even walking if all your clients are located close to your home and to one another. You'd certainly get fit! But mobile hairdressers also have a lot to carry, so most rely on a car to be able to do business.

Health Insurance will protect you against being unable to work due to illness. Allegedly. This is how the policies are sold, and the people who sell them make a lot of money out of your fear. If you find a policy that seems a fair price, read the small print very, very carefully. Then read it again. Many have so many clauses and conditions it is impossible to work out under what set of circumstances they would actually pay out.

Equipment Insurance will protect your equipment such as hairdryers, scissors, clippers etc against loss through theft or damage. But before investing in such a policy, check out your house contents and car insurance – you might find you are already covered.

BUSINESS NAMES

What to call your new business? It is easy to get completely side-tracked by this question and spend hours or days thinking up clever combinations. Really, you have two options: think of a snazzy name for your business or just use your own name. Let's look at the benefits and drawbacks of each:

Curl Up And Dye
Yes, this really is the name of a salon. Catchy or ridiculous – you decide. One thing is certain, you won't forget it in a

hurry! The good thing about a name for business is that you can choose one which will stand out. It can be one that makes clients laugh or makes them cringe. It can be classy or cheesy. You can pick a name that does exactly what it says on the tin, like *Hair At Home*, or something a little more obscure.

If you choose a name for your business that is other than your own name you would be advised to register it. Your business's name is important. It is how people remember you, what they see in your advertising, your leaflets, business cards and stationery. It's also how your business gets recommended to others.

Registering your business name will allow you protection against other hairdressers 'passing off' under your name. If you haven't registered your name there is nothing to stop someone else starting up a business using the same name – potentially losing you a lot of business.

Case study:
Maria had been running Hair & Now for eight years. She had built a clientele from nothing and enjoyed her work, which consisted largely of servicing the older population of her town.

One day she noticed an advert in the local paper for another mobile hairdressing service. Maria says: 'The advert was for a company called Hair And Now – exactly the same as mine apart from using the word And instead of the symbol. I was so shocked. I just stared at it and didn't know what to do.'

Maria was right to be upset. There was every chance that this new business would be able to capitalize on the solid reputation she herself had built up under the name Hair & Now.

Sure enough, Maria started to notice a drop in the number of referrals she was receiving.

'Loads of my clients said they were recommending me, but I wasn't getting many calls! It seems the new clients were looking in the paper, seeing this advert and calling them instead.'

Because Maria hadn't protected her business name there was very little she could do. The owner of the other business refused to change their name. Maria re-launched her business with a new name – which is now registered and protected.

The National Business Register has lots on information on its website:

http://www.nationalbusinessregister.co.uk/business_names/

When choosing a name for your business, it is worth considering whether you intend to also have a website. If you do, it is wise to check the availability of a suitable domain name before you settle on a business name – just in case there isn't one free. The National Business Register can search for you, or you can visit any of the web hosting services such as www.123reg.co.uk or www.1and1.com

If you find a name you are happy with and the domain is available, snap it up before somebody else does – even if you think it will be a while before you get your website up and running.

FINANCING YOUR BUSINESS

How much money will you need to set up a mobile hairdressing business? This will depend on a lot of factors, including how much money you need to live off every month (if you live with parents or a partner who can support you for a while

you would obviously need less than a single person with a huge mortgage).

Other factors will be; whether you have an existing client base to work with (less money spent on initial advertising), whether you already have a car or need to buy one, how much equipment you already have and the condition it is in, and how good the demographics are for hairdressing in your area (details about the population and their needs).

In the next section, **Planning**, you will find out exactly how much you need to get started and survive the initial stages of self-employment. Then you can decide on how you are going to raise the money – from your own savings, from family, or from a bank.

Using your own savings is obviously the easiest, and safest, option. The risk is entirely your own, and there is no need to go cap-in-hand to anyone else to ask for help. If you are planning on opening your own mobile hairdressing business at some point in the future, start saving NOW. If you are ready to take the plunge but your bank account is empty, the next best option is probably borrowing from your family.

Never mix family and business is a wise saying, but it is also a lot less scary to be indebted to people who (hopefully) aren't going to take you to court if you miss a few payments due to illness or some other catastrophe. Assess your options. Who is likely to a) have the money spare and not need it back within at least a year, and b) be likely to say yes without giving you a really hard time. If there is no one in your family who fits this bill (and many family members don't), your last option is to go to your bank.

This is where you want to have a really good record with your bank. Any previous borrowing should be paid back on time

every month. Credit cards should be spent on wisely and up to date with payments. You will also need a really great business plan – see the next two sections, *Planning and Putting Together A Business Plan* for a fool-proof guide to this.

However you finance your business, make sure you are comfortable with your choices. DO NOT ever borrow more than you can pay back, and watch out for those interest rates. Remember to factor the repayments into your survival budget. If at all possible, finance the start-up of your business yourself – even if it means waiting just a little longer to get going.

THE COMPETITION

A very important consideration before you get started is the competition in your local area – and this doesn't only mean mobile hairdressers. Salons are also in competition with you for clients, and they have something you can't offer. You will no doubt be able to beat them on price, but, as we will see a little later, you would be unwise to set your prices too low. So assess the competition carefully. Get hold of your local paper and the yellow pages and make a few notes on the following points:

A. How many salons are there in your town/city/village?

B. How many mobile hairdressers? (Bear in mind that many successful mobile hairdressers no longer need to advertise so there may be others you don't know about.)

C. Phone a selection and ask for prices

D. Try a few of them out for yourself – yes, you can risk it!

E. Is there a particular concentration of hairdressers in one or two areas?

F. Likewise, are there any area which aren't well served by salons or mobiles?

G. From the advertising and prices, who do you think each salon or mobile service is aimed at? (Known as their target market.)

These notes will help you later when you come to put together your business plan. For now they should give you some idea of what you're up against.

TIP: *A lack of any competition at all is not always a good sign – it can mean there is no call for the service in that area. If this were the case, further research would be necessary to establish a need – by canvassing, for example.*

JOINING A PROFESSIONAL ORGANISATION

Before you start out on your own, you may want to consider joining a professional organisation, such as the Freelance Hair and Beauty Federation. Membership is not expensive and can open many doors, as well as get you discounts on insurance, products and training. An organisation such as this often has local groups who meet and share stories and experiences – a useful way of combating the loneliness we discussed earlier.

There will be other, local organisations you could join, such as the Chamber of Commerce; a useful way of gaining contacts and local business. Keep an eye out for opportunities to make connections with other business people.

PERSONAL SAFETY

The last, and perhaps most important, consideration when starting up a mobile hairdressing business is your own safety.

You will be going into the houses of complete strangers – at least initially before you have built up a round of regular clients. Some of these people will have been recommended, others will have called you from your adverts or leaflets. Others may have arranged the appointment by email – you will never have even spoken to them. Ninety-nine percent of the time they will be lovely, genuine people who'll make you a cup of tea and place themselves in your capable hands.

But what will you do if they are not?

Maybe this is of more concern to female hairdressers than to men. Or maybe not. Male stylists will be just as vulnerable to theft or aggression. This section will aim its advice to hairdressers of both sexes, but if you are a man and some of it doesn't apply to you please just disregard the advice and read on.

There are several ways you can protect yourself as a mobile hairdresser visiting clients in their homes, and it would be wise to make the following steps part of your everyday system for taking and keeping appointments:

1. Only ever take bookings over the phone from new clients. If a client contacts you via email, ask for her number and call her to arrange the appointment, or to ask for directions.

2. Only take bookings from women (one for the ladies only, perhaps). If a gentleman calls and says he would like to book you to do his wife's hair, ask politely if you could speak to his wife first. By all means, have men as clients! But until you know them, make sure their wife, daughter or partner will be at the house the first time you visit.

3. Make the cost of service crystal clear, and let the client know how you would like to be paid. Do this when the

appointment is booked. For first-time clients you could ask for cash.

4. Don't carry a lot of cash with you. Get into the habit of popping to the bank to pay any large sums in, or drop in at home and leave it in a safe place there. Have a money belt, and keep cash in a separate section, so if you are looking for change no one can see wads of notes.

5. Trust your instincts. If you arrive at a house and feel uncomfortable – at any time, even if you haven't gone in yet – leave immediately.

To begin with you will spread your net far and wide, and will attract clients of all types. You may find yourself in situations you don't feel happy with – while another person might be fine in the same situation. YOU have to feel comfortable as well as the client. If you're not, just leave. Don't ask for your money, just go.

Case study:
Susan had been in business for three months when a man called, answering her advert in the paper. He asked if she would come to his house and give his wife a colour. Susan asked if she could speak to the wife to discuss the colour. The man told her that it was a surprise for her birthday.

'I said I needed to know which colours to bring with me,' says Susan, 'as I don't carry a lot of stock. The man said blonde, which didn't really help much.'

Susan suggested the man tell his wife about the surprise and then asked her to call Susan with her requirements.

'That was when he started to get quite aggressive. He kept saying "Just come over here and you'll see", which sounded a bit ominous to me.'

Susan, now quite suspicious, refused to go, but said she was happy to do his wife's hair with a little bit more information from her. She never heard from the man or his wife.

'I still don't know if it was genuine or not, but I wasn't willing to take the risk. Sometimes you just have to trust your instincts.'

PLANNING

Why Plan?
So, you don't want to waste time planning and are eager to just get going with your business. That is one way of going ahead but remember the old saying – those who fail to plan, plan to fail!

Planning can be fun. You are setting out into the unknown, embarking on an exciting adventure. How much better the journey will be if you have a map to guide you, to make sure you actually reach your destination.

Another reason to plan is if you are going to need financial help setting up your business. Even if you intend to approach family or friends for a loan it won't hurt to show them you are serious about your venture. If you are going to try your luck with a bank for finance a business plan will be vital.

Know Where You're Going - Setting Targets
During the first six months to one year of being in business you are understandably focussed on one thing only – earning money. Without it there is no point in getting up in the morning, after all, you're not a charity. But there comes a time in the lifetime of every business where things seem to grind to a halt of their own accord. This happens sooner, and is more damaging, in businesses which had no initial plan.

Think of it like this – you start off in a flurry of advertising, excitedly telling everyone you meet about your wonderful new business. You get a few clients. They tell some of their friends about you and – hey presto! – you have a clientele.

Trouble is, you kept your prices deliberately low to attract these clients and after a few months you realise you are working really hard but can't actually afford to pay your bills. You decide to put your prices up – surely your loyal, happy clients won't mind.

Unfortunately they do mind. And they leave you in droves. What you didn't realise was, they were only attracted to you because of your low prices. Quality, experience, and your sparkling personality were just an added bonus. These clients will always follow the cheapest price – that's a fact of hairdressing life. YOU should have been chasing a different type of client altogether, but you didn't realise this because (you guessed it) you didn't make a plan.

Planning will tell you a number of essential things:

• How much money you need to turn over in order to survive and pay your bills. Turnover is not the same as profit (and profit is what you can pay yourself out of). You will have expenses and costs, national insurance and tax, and all sorts of things to pay out of the money you receive from clients.

• How many appointments you need in any given week in order to break even, and the minimum you will have to charge for those appointments.

• Who else is doing the same as you in your area – the competition. What are they charging, how successful are they, are they any good? Don't know the answers to these questions? You should.

PUTTING TOGETHER A BUSINESS PLAN

Your business plan can be anything you want it to be, from a fairly official document (like the one shown below) to just a few notes on a scrap of paper. The point is for YOU to know where you are going – and how you are going to get there.

The following business plan is included to show you what one is supposed to look like, as most people setting up in business for the first time have never seen one before. You could use this as a model for your own plan, simply inserting your own name, business name, and other relevant information where appropriate.

This business plan is intended to help secure funding for the start up of a new mobile hairdressing business called Hair 2 U. Some of the figures are quite complicated, but if you can grasp and follow them you're well on your way to being a successful entrepreneur.

Sample Business Plan

Business Plan
prepared for
Hair 2 U

1. Summary
This is a new business venture for YOUR NAME. The business will be operated as a sole-trader and began trading on INSERT DATE.

Hair 2 U will provide a mobile hairdressing service. The idea behind Hair 2 U is to 'bring the salon into people's homes', providing all towels, products, and a professional salon-style service.

Hair 2 U has the benefit of an established clientele and an

owner/manager who has worked for ten years in top salons.

The plan covers the following areas; Nature and history of the business, Management of the business, Sales and marketing, Product and services, Insurance, Financial planning – profit and loss, Monitoring performance – cash flow forecast, Personal survival budget, Assessing profitability, Contingency/risk assessment.

2. Nature and history of the Business

Hair 2 U offers a full hairdressing service, catering for individuals and families, visiting people in their homes in the area.

The business is based on the idea that there is a market for a professional, customer orientated hairdressing service for people in their homes. Clients benefit from having all the factors usually present in a salon environment; qualified and insured stylists, all products provided, towels provided, a relaxing experience, feeling pampered, without the stress/time/costs/parking worries of visiting a salon.

The business will commence on INSERT DATE and be operated as a sole-trader.

No licence is needed to operate. YOUR NAME is a fully qualified hairdresser, having served a formal apprenticeship. He/she is a member of the Freelance Hair and Beauty Federation for support and credibility.

Aims and Objectives for Year

PERSONAL AIMS AND OBJECTIVES	BUSINESS AIMS AND OBJECTIVES
To gain a reputation for excellent customer service and quality work. To draw a salary equal to £20k pa.	To turnover £25k. To gain regular, loyal clients.

3. Management of the Business

INSERT CV OR WORK EXPERIENCE HERE.

Strengths:
- Knowledge and experience of meeting and exceeding client's needs and expectations

- Excellent hairdressing skills

- Good listener

- Hard working

- Good writing skills, for writing promotional material etc

- Good computer skills

- Open minded

- Creative

Skills needed to take the business forward:

SKILLS REQUIRED	✓
Cutting, colouring and perming	✓
Putting hair up	✓
Fashion techniques	✓
Marketing skills	✓
Customer service skills	✓
Book keeping	✓
Accounting	Self-assessment online
Goal setting	✓
Investing profits	Advice from bank
Web site design	Outsource

4. SALES AND MARKETING

The Market

The market is currently increasing; hair and beauty expenditure has increased over the last decade to 2.55 billion (source: Office for National Statistics).

Demographics affect the market, and the fall in 15-19 year olds and 20-24 year olds may affect the market. It is anticipated that there will also be a fall in 25-34 year olds, while the 35+ group will increase.

The increasing number of working women will have a positive impact on the size of the market. Also, the increasing emphasis on appearance in today's society means more regular visits to the hairdressers and a willingness to spend more on their hair.

Locally, the size of the market is assumed to be large, with a growing population, and the area is being developed and expanded.

Target customer groups

• Women with a disposable income, at home in the daytime, to whom appearance is important. They appreciate quality and are happy to pay for it. Age approx 20 – 55.

• Women who work and have a disposable income, to whom appearance is important. Will like to have their hair done at home for the convenience.

• Women with families, i.e. children at home, and like to have a mobile hairdresser for the convenience of having the whole family's hair done in one go at home.

All the above are regular clients, having their hair done every 4-6 weeks. For simplicity the calculations for the sales

forecasts have been based on a cycle of 6 weeks for all clients, while recognizing that in reality a greater frequency will have a positive effect on the business.

- Hair 2 U caters for men, but for security reasons only accepts bookings from women and only cuts gents hair alongside a ladies haircut.

- OAP's who have a shampoo and set are not catered for due to lack of equipment.

- Families are welcomed and encouraged.

Services Offered

Mobile hairdressing services including; cutting, colouring, hi-lights, perms, styling, putting hair up, children's and gent's hair, full consultation and advice on styling and maintenance.

Hair 2 U will bring the salon into people's homes by providing a quality, salon-standard hairdressing service. This means that all products (shampoo, conditioners, styling products etc) are provided, as are towels, gowns, and equipment (hairdryers, brushes).

USPs

FEATURES	BENEFIT TO CLIENT
Bringing the salon into the home	Convenience
Over 10 years experience	Reassuring, can have confidence they are in safe hands
Fully insured	Again, reassuring; knowledge of being protected
Reliable	
Professional	Never inconvenienced by hairdresser not turning up
All products and towels provided	Inspires confidence

FEATURES	BENEFIT TO CLIENT
Advice on maintenance (leaflets given to clients who have had a perm or a colour)	No fuss or hassle, just sit down and relax
	Able to care for their own hair and keep the style themselves
Evenings and weekends	
Up to date skills and services	Convenience
	Can obtain the most up to date styles

Customers will use Hair 2 U rather than a competitor because they are recommended by friends and colleagues, attracted in the first instance by the professional image of the business and all enquiries are dealt with promptly, professionally Customers will use Hair 2 U rather than a competitor because they are recommended by friends and colleagues, attracted in the first instance by the professional image of the business and all enquiries are dealt with promptly, professionally and with genuine interest. They continue to use the service because they have experienced the quality of hairdressing for themselves and trust and feel comfortable with YOUR NAME, who listens to them and gives them the hairstyle they want.

The weaknesses of the mobile hairdressing business are; a) some people do prefer to visit a salon, and b) YOUR NAME can't carry a large stock and can't be as responsive as a salon could be.

COMPETITION

Other Mobile hairdressers

INSERT DETAILS OF OTHER MOLBILE HAIRDRESSERS IN

YOUR AREA HERE.

Salons
INSERT DETAILS OF LOCAL SALONS HERE.

SALES AND PROMOTION

Trading name
The trading name of Hair 2 U reflects the modern, professional image of the business. The name also tells people exactly what the business does.

Seasonal variations
The quieter times of the year are July/August and January/February. Promotional activities are run prior to these times to encourage clients to recommend friends and family, and to tempt them to try something new, for example a colour or a perm.

The busiest time of year is Christmas, and extra advertising at this time capitalizes on this and helps build a larger clientele; also, promotional activities run at this time improve sales in the coming quieter period of January.

Promoting the business
1. Hair 2 U will advertise in the local paper to gain initial clients

2. Leaflets will be produced to give to local organizations to promote the business

3. Hair 2 U will be listed in free web directories and in the Yellow Pages

4. Hair 2 U will have its own website which is currently in development

Marketing activities are monitored on an excel spreadsheet, giving all activities a source code and asking clients where they heard about Hair 2 U. The results will be analyzed to ensure that the marketing budget is being used efficiently.

PRICES

Competitor prices

SERVICE	COMPETITOR ONE	COMPETITOR TWO
Cut and blow dry	£20.00	£15.00
Wet cut	-	£10.00
Hi lights (cap) inc. CBD	£30.00	£28.00
Hi lights (foil or mesh) inc. CBD	£45.00	-
Full head tint inc. CBD	£40.00	£33.00
Perm inc. CBD	-	£30.00
Gents (Trim)	-	£5.00

Prices for Hair 2 U

SERVICE	HAIR 2 U PRICES
Cut and blow dry	From £20.00
Wet cut	From £15.00
Hi lights (cap) inc. CBD	From £40.00
Hi lights (foil) inc. CBD	From £50.00
Full head tint inc. CBD	From £40.00
Perm inc. CBD	From £50.00
Gents (Trim)	£7.00*
Under 14s	From £5.00*

*Only available with another service due to travelling costs and time

Hair 2 U's prices reflect the results of research into how much people are prepared to pay for mobile hairdressing services, and also take into account the competition, overheads and cost of materials, and the breakeven figure.

5. PRODUCTS AND SERVICES

The comprehensive list of services to be provided is as follows; cut and blow dry, wet cut, hi-lights with a cap, hi-lights/low-lights using foil, tinting, perming, putting hair up, bridal hair, hair advice and consultation.

It is not the intention of Hair 2 U to sell any products at this time, although this may be introduced at a later date.

Suppliers
Hair 2 U has formed a relationship with A Hairdressing Supplies for the usable stock and most of the equipment. They are open on Sundays. An account has not been set up yet but will be in the future.

6. EQUIPMENT AND VEHICLES

Equipment
Equipment owned and used by the business; scissors, brushes, clippers, hairdryer, gowns, towels, bag, colour chart, style book, mixing bowls, measuring jug, hi-lighting cap, perm rollers, plug and play heat gun, sample hair, promotional materials.

Hairdryer and clippers generally need replacing once a year, and scissors will need replacing after three years.

Vehicle
The business vehicle is a *INSERT VEHICLE HERE*, owned by

YOUR NAME and valued at *VALUE*. The vehicle is in good working order and is serviced regularly.

7. INSURANCE

Public liability insurance is provided via the Freelance Hair and Beauty Federation (example provider).

The vehicle insurers have been informed of the change of use of the vehicle.

Personal insurance, to cover periods of ill-health, will be looked into.

8. PROFIT AND LOSS ACCOUNT

Please see appendix 1. (Sample of a profit and loss account in *Further Resources*.)

9. CASH FLOW FORECAST

Please see appendix 2. (Sample of a cash flow forecast in *Further Resources*.)

10. PERSONAL SURVIVAL BUDGET

Estimated expenditure

	£ MONTHLY
Mortgage/Rent	650
Council tax & water	120
Gas & electricity	50
Property insurances	30
Food, general housekeeping expenses	350

Clothes	50
Entertainment (meals, drinks)	50
National insurance	30
Total survival income	1330

11. ASSESSING PROFITABILITY

Variable costs have been determined as usable stock only, all other costs are fixed.

FIXED COSTS	£ ANNUALLY
Fuel	1000
MOT	100
Car tax	200
Car maintenance/servicing	200
Car insurance	300
Advertising/marketing	500
Home phone	300
Mobile phone	240
Equipment	75
Stationary/printing	150
Electricity	60
Training	100
Clothing	100
Public liability insurance	95
Drawings (basic survival budget)	15960
Total	19380

Profitability Calculations

8 hours x 5 days = 40 hours/week x 46 weeks = 1,920 hours
(allowing for 4 weeks per year holiday/sickness)

Working on 75% of total productive hours (1,920) = 1,440
Total hours = 1,440

Fixed costs of £19,380 divided by 1,440 hours = **£13.45 per hour minimum charge**

Total sales expected = £25,000
Total variable costs = £2,500 (generally 10% of sales)
Total fixed costs = £19,380

Gross profit (sales – variable costs) = £22,500
Gross margin (gross profit / sales) = 90%
Pre-tax profit (gross profit – fixed costs) = £3,120
Breakeven sales (fixed costs / gross margin %) = £17,442

12. CONTINGENCY/RISK ASSESSMENT

Assumptions have been made in this business plan based on previous knowledge of the industry and current market research. It is more of a possibility that sales will be higher than anticipated. However, advertising and marketing costs could also be greater than forecasted.

In this event the business would fall back on extra profits.

Another circumstance which could change is if the proprietor suffered ill health. The strains of the business (long hours, irregular eating habits) could contribute to this. Every step will be taken to keep healthy, and an insurance policy will be purchased to cover outgoings such as the mortgage in the event of unforeseeable ill health.

Attached
Appendix 1: Profit and loss account
Appendix 2: Cash flow forecast

WHICH SERVICES TO OFFER

As you will be running your own mobile salon, the choice of services to offer is completely yours. Will you offer just hair-cuts, cutting down on equipment, stock and expenses but also limiting your clientele? Or will you go for the full range of hairdressing services to rival any salon? Will you specialize in perming – handy if most of your clients love a perm and a shampoo and set?

Most mobile hairdressers offer most services, and a few offer additional services such as hair extensions or beauty treatments. Whatever you decide, it is important you are properly trained and use only safe and reliable stock. Don't, for example, buy your perming lotions cheap in bulk. This may be okay for certain salons, particularly if they get through vats of it a week. You will have to store all your supplies at home, and use them within their sell-by dates.

Let's take a look at each of the services in turn:

Hair cutting

A given for any hairdresser, and the backbone of the mobile's income. Cuts for ladies, gents and children will form the greatest part of your business, and other services can be added on as needed. The great thing about a haircut is it needs nothing other than you and your scissors and comb – and maybe a gown, water-spray, razor, floor-covering, neck-brush, clippers, section grips...

See how easy it is to get bogged down with equipment!

Try to be flexible and receptive with your haircuts. If a neigh-bour pops in while you're doing one client's hair and asks for a trim don't book her in for another day – do it right there and then. If it is going to make you very late for your next client

(more than fifteen minutes), call your client and explain. Opportunities like this are a great way to gain new clients, as well as a reputation for being flexible.

TIP: *Always allow yourself an extra ten or fifteen minutes between appointments to allow for traffic or for unexpected problems. Clients can chat for England! (And so can most hairdressers!) It's easy to get caught up in a conversation then find yourself late for every appointment for rest of the day.*

It is worth considering offering a package that includes floor-coverings, towels, shampoos and blow-drys to clients who want a haircut. Not only does it make you look far more professional than other mobile hairdressers, it makes it easy for the client to have you in her home. Most people cite 'mess' as a reason NOT to use a mobile hairdresser. Solve this problem for them before it becomes a problem. It's no trouble to carry a small dust-pan and brush and offer to sweep up the hair. Most clients will say no, but the fact that you offered goes a long way.

Blow-drying

Which brings us on to blow-drys. These can be offered as a service on their own, or only as an add-on, or finisher, for other services. One thing to consider when deciding how to offer blow-drys will be how much you can reasonably charge for one. If it is too high then few people will be able to see the value in booking you – and this could affect their decision to book you for other services as well, even if these offer better value.

But – if you don't charge enough for your blow-drys, you could find that once you've factored in fuel costs, and your own time, you are actually giving them away for free!

Colouring

Hi-lights, low-lights, tints, semi-permanents – all these are fantastic revenue-making services for the mobile hairdresser. You will need an up-to-date shade chart, and at least three mixing bowls and applicator brushes. Foils or meche, for hi-lights and low-lights, and possibly a hi-lighting cap and hook. If you offer colouring you will definitely need to take some kind of floor covering with you to protect your client's flooring. And towels, cotton wool, a measuring jug, and a protective gown (plus a spare in case it gets splashed).

One of the best ways to make money out of colouring is to have another haircut to do while the colour is processing. This could be your client's husband, friend, neighbour, or even children. Otherwise you will be sitting around drinking coffee while the colour takes – nice, of course, but not earning you any money. It could be worth offering a price incentive to your colour client, 10% off for example, if they invite a friend to have a haircut while you are there. You will still make more money than you would have otherwise – and you now have a new client!

Always do the mixing of colours in your client's kitchen, near to their sink, and wash out bowls and brushes as soon as you have finished. It's surprising how easy it is for tint bowls to get knocked off surfaces in the average household with kids and pets around. Put everything away as you go so you don't leave anything behind.

Perming

So far you have limited yourself to a reasonable manageable amount of equipment and stock to carry. If you want to offer perming to your clients you will need to up this by about fifty percent. Rollers of many different sizes, perm lotion, end-papers, neutraliser, LOTS of towels, plastic caps, and some

means of processing the perm, such as an overhead dryer.

Consider that not everyone has a driveway, or somewhere you can park your car right outside. Many live in flats, or terraces, or other places that could incur a fairly lengthy walk. The more equipment you have to carry the harder your job will be. If over thirty percent of your clients regularly have perms it is easily worth investing in the equipment, and putting in the extra effort. If not, think about declining to offer this service.

Hair-up and Wedding hair

Another money-spinner, this. If you have the necessary skills (and you do need the skills – being able to do a French pleat is not enough), you can earn in excess of £300 a day during the wedding season. Proms are becoming more popular, and prom hair is another way of marketing your services. The other benefit of hair-ups is the complete lack of equipment – other than clips and a comb, and lots of hairspray, it is just you and your skills that are needed.

Hair extensions

A very popular service amongst certain types of clients – if you live in an area heavily populated by WAGs you are laughing! But extensions, or add-ins, are not just for those who want flowing locks. Add-ins can be used for extra volume, or for adding colour to clients who are a little chemical shy. Companies such as Balmain offer training and add-in products that can be marketed and inserted quickly and easily.

Do get proper training. There are far too many horror stories about hair extensions gone wrong for you to even attempt to offer this service without it. When booking extensions, always take a deposit from the client. You will have to order and buy the hair, which you will probably not be able to use

on another client if they cancel. Many companies don't take returns on hair. So make sure your deposit covers any out of pocket costs, as well as a portion of your valuable time.

Thinking About Your Target Market

Who will your clients be? Saying 'people who want their hair cut' isn't quite enough. Ask yourself the following questions:

- Why will your clients choose you instead of another hairdresser?

- Assuming they already have their hair done elsewhere, why will they change to you?

- What will you offer that is special or different and why will this appeal?

- Where will your clients live?

- How old will they be? (An age range is fine.)

- How much disposable income do they have? Are they fairly well off or on a tight budget?

- How much free time do they have? Are they at work in the day, or at home with young children?

- Are your clients likely to be the loyal type, who will come back again and again, or the type to follow the cheapest price?

- What kind of services will they want from you and how often?

You get the picture. You need to build up a profile of your ideal client, based on your location and the people who live in your area.

Why bother? Why not just place an advert and get on with answering the phone? For one thing, you will need to have

an idea who your clients are going to be before you can even decide where to place the advert. What papers do they read, or which shops/community centre/leisure facilities will they be likely to visit. What kind of design will appeal to them? An advert aimed at working mothers will be very different, in design and location, to one aimed at young men about town.

> **Consider this:** Deciding on your target clients will also help you to decide which ranges of products to use, helping with your budgeting.

SETTING PRICES

Setting your prices will be one of the most important things you do when starting out on your own. Too high and you will put off certain clients and lose business. Too low and you risk not making a profit at all. One thing to remember is that you can always lower your prices, with discounts or special offers, but it is very hard to increase them by any margin other than a natural, inflation-driven amount.

To set your prices there are two main factors to consider: the competition and your overheads. Let's look at each in turn.

The Competition

Thanks to the research you did earlier, you should now have some pretty extensive notes about the competition. If you didn't phone at least two salons and tow mobile hairdressers, do it now. Note the prices of all the services you are planning to offer. Make a chart like the one shown in part 4 of the sample business plan.

TIP: *While you are on the phone, assess how professional the hairdresser or salon sounds. Are they polite, or harassed and rushed? Do they answer the phone within a reasonable amount of rings? Ask about availability – are they booked solid or do they have spaces?*

Look at your research. Where do you see your prices sitting compared to the competition. If the competition is very strong, i.e. offering services you can't or a lot more experienced, you may want to come in slightly lower. If the local mobile services and salons are weaker, you should start your prices at the same level. Remember, you can always lower them if it is difficult getting clients.

Your Costs

If you have started to produce your own business plan along the lines of the sample one offered, you will already have a good idea of your costs, including your survival budget and your break-even figures. This will give you a figure that you must charge equal to or more than:

In our example, Hair 2 U, the profitability calculations were as follows:

8 hours x 5 days = 40 hours/week x 48 weeks = 1,920 hours
(allowing for 4 weeks per year holiday/sickness)
Working on 75% of total productive hours (1,920) = 1,440
Total hours = 1,440

Fixed costs of £19,380 divided by 1,440 hours = £13.45 per hour minimum charge

Let's look at this in a little more detail. First, we are assuming that the hairdresser is working for 8 hours a day, for 5 days of the week. This equals 40 hours a week. So far so good. We multiply this by 48 weeks. Why not 52? Because even super-hardworking hairdressers need time to recharge occasionally. And get sick. So we have assumed 4 weeks of the year for holidays or sickness. This gives us 1,920 hours worked over an average year!

So what does 75% of productive hours mean? It is quite simple – it assumes that you will not always be fully booked

for 100% of your 40 hours a week. There may be down-times and empty slots. In fact, when you are first starting out you may find that you are only busy for 25% of your productive hours! We are being cautiously optimistic with our business plan, and opting for 75% productivity.

Multiplying our total yearly hours of 1,920 by 75% gives us a total of 1,440 hours we believe will be full of clients paying us money!

Next comes our costs. In the example, our assumptions were as follows:

FIXED COSTS	£ ANNUALLY
Fuel	1000
MOT	100
Car tax	200
Car maintenance/servicing	200
Car insurance	300
Advertising/marketing	500
Home phone	300
Mobile phone	240
Equipment	75
Stationary/printing	150
Electricity	60
Training	100
Clothing	100
Public liability insurance	95
Drawings (basic survival)budget)	15960
Total	19380

Of course, these are assumptions. But all planning is based on what we imagine will happen. Your figures may be very different, and your best guess is absolutely fine.

Including our imaginary survival budget, this puts our fixed costs at £19,380 for the year. This may seem high, but in our example the hairdresser has a house to run, on her own.

The next step is a simple one – divide your fixed costs (£19,380) by the number of productive hours (1,440), giving you a figure that you absolutely must earn to break even. In this case, that figure is £13.45.

This means that Hair 2 U must charge at least £13.45 per hour. They can charge more, if the competition indicates that a higher charge will be sustained, but they cannot charge less without seriously risking not being able to meet their own financial needs or that of the business.

So what does this mean in practice? If you are booking appointments in hourly, with one hour allocated to a haircut, for example, you must charge at least £13.45 for that hair-cut. If you were able to complete two haircuts in one hour (allowing for travelling between clients this would be tricky) you could charge a minimum of £7 per haircut. If, however, due to your location you could only manage one haircut per hour and a half (if your clients were spread out all across the countryside, for instance), you would have to charge them at least £21 for a haircut in order to break even.

Do you find these figures confusing and irritating or exciting and empowering? Aim to feel excited about figures like this because they are your FRIEND not your enemy. Your calcula-tions will make the difference between a thriving business that brings you a more than satisfactory income for years, and a failed venture that leaves you puzzled and sore.

CHOOSING PRODUCTS

Unless you are only offering a hair cutting service, you will need to use a range, or a number of ranges, of products on your clients. In fact, even if you are only cutting hair, you may be required to shampoo occasionally, or blow-dry. You could use your client's own products, of course, but ask yourself – what does that say about you as a professional hairdresser?

It says that you think your client knows more about what's good for their hair than you do!

This isn't the case (hopefully), so raise yourself above other mobile hairdressers by choosing and using a good range of products every time you visit a client. The products don't have to be expensive, or even exclusive, they just need to something your clients can't get their hands on in their local chemist or supermarket.

Obviously you will need to find a supplier for your usable stock – items like tubes of tint, peroxide, perm lotions etc. But wholesalers also sell shampoos, conditioners, styling product, brushes, and much more.

The reasons for using good products on your client's hair are the same for any salon. Firstly, their hair will be a finer texture, and in better condition, and therefore look even more fantastic, earning your clients compliments – and you more business!

The second reason is that you can sell the products to your clients. Clients buy their hair products from salons all the time. Or, they buy them from supermarkets. Why shouldn't they buy from you? When you style your fantastic haircut, make a big deal out of the styling products you are using. Your client will want to recreate the look themselves – and will ask you where they can buy them.

Take some time choosing your product range. The whole-sale price will be important, as you will have to consider your mark-up (the amount you add on to sell to the client) to ensure you make at least a small profit. Remember to add VAT – most wholesalers add VAT to the bill at check-out, so the shelf price won't include this.

Setting Up An Account

Many wholesalers will allow you to set up an account – although some will want you to have been in business for a while and to have a minimum monthly order. Buying your sup-plies this way improves your cash-flow no end. The whole-saler will give you at least thirty days to settle your account, leaving your cash free to clear bills or pay expenses.

Larger wholesalers, such as Sally Hair and Beauty or Aston and Fincher may not be willing to consider an account, but many smaller wholesalers will. Whatever the situation, it doesn't hurt to ask.

CHAPTER THREE
BUILDING UP YOUR BUSINESS

Now you are up and running, how will you build your business from a fledgling venture to a mighty enterprise?

In this section we will look at a number of strategies for growing your business, including referrals, advertising – paid-for and free, discounts, talks and demonstrations, and having a website. We will also look at ways to keep track of what works – and what doesn't.

Throughout this section keep in mind the following statement:

"If your business isn't growing, it's shrinking."

In fact, you would be wise to keep this in mind always. Businesses have a natural rate of attrition. Clients move away, they get bored, they decide to grow their hair and don't call for a while, they stray elsewhere, they suddenly get a best friend who's a hairdresser! Basically, you are going to be losing clients through no fault of your own – and there is nothing you can do about it. Except, perhaps, constantly be looking for new ones...

REFERRALS

The quickest – and cheapest – way to find new clients is through referrals from your existing clients. Not only does this save on advertising costs, the new clients are already 'pre-sold'; they already feel confident in your abilities and professionalism. There is also a good chance they know how much you charge, your availability, and how you like to work.

Referrals are also an incredibly affirming gesture. Someone is saying, 'You are really good at hairdressing and I want to try you out.' Wow! What better feeling could there be than that?

Encouraging Clients to Make Referrals

So how exactly do you get your clients to refer you to their friends, family, co-workers, neighbours – or even people they chat to in the supermarket queue? By making them exceptionally happy with their hair, that's how.

It has been said that when a client or customer is unhappy with a service they will tell on average twenty people! But when they are happy they will tell only two. This seems incredibly unfair. Obviously, you must make sure your clients aren't unhappy, that goes without saying. But how do you up the number of people they tell, and increase the chances of one of those people calling you up?

There are various methods you can use, and the most simple – and effective – is merely to ask! That's right. Just saying to your clients "Please will you recommend me to your friends" works very well most of the time. You can make it a lot easier by giving each client a stock of business cards to hand out to their friends and family. This way they don't have to search around for your phone number when someone compliments them on their fantastic hairstyle.

Another method many hairdressers use to encourage referrals is by using incentives. These can work in many different ways, but the basis is that you offer either a discount or a free service in return for a certain number of referrals. Always make the conditions of the incentive very clear to your clients, and ALWAYS deliver the incentive as soon as the referred client has used your services.

TIP: *An example of a good incentive scheme is to hand out a certain number of cards to a client (three is a good number) and ask them to write their name and address on the back of the card before they give the card to a friend. The referred friend must then give you the card when she has her hair done. (Make sure you have another set of three cards to give to the new client!)*

When you have received two of the three cards from one particular client you can reduce their next service by ten percent, or give them a free blow-dry or bottle of shampoo – whatever you feel would be a suitable reward for that client. Some clients will value money off, others won't. Some like a free gift, others prefer a reduced price. Some clients will even refuse the incentive, happy just to recommend you. But by offering it you are being proactive and making it easy and worthwhile for your clients to refer you.

Friends and Family
Your own friends and family have an important role to play in the building of your business. They will be (hopefully) happy to help in any way they can. Start by giving each friend or family member a stack of cards and asking them to hand them out to their own friends, colleagues, people they talk to at the gym, in shops – anywhere they can.

It may be worth offering to cut your friends and family's hair at a discounted price to encourage them to help refer you.

Not only is this a nice and generous gesture, it also allows them to quite honestly say – Yes, she is really good!

TIP: *Never offer to do your family or friends' hair for free. Even if you have done so in the past. Even if they are broke. Never. You are running a business; this is your livelihood. Your friends and family must respect this and learn not to take advantage. You might think you don't mind now, but at some point in the future, when you are working flat out and you need a little down-time, you will be annoyed by having to take your scissors with you every time you visit Aunty Eileen on your day off. Charge at least a nominal fee so that they take your business and your time seriously.*

There may be people in your social circle or family with whom you could have a reciprocal arrangement. These are the only circumstances where you could do someone's hair for no charge – no financial charge, that is. If a friend happens to be an accountant, for example, they could offer to do your end-of-year accounts in return for hairdressing. (Find out how much this would cost you in cash from another accountant and only offer an equal number of haircuts. It is no good if the accounting service is worth £200 and you offer a years' worth of colouring worth £400.)

Other skills and services you could utilize amongst friends and family include: Web design, marketing skills, car repairs, printing, logo design, and babysitting. And, of course, hairdressing! Hairdressers need to look great too.

ADVERTISING – FREE AND PAID FOR

Advertising is the backbone of most businesses, but for hairdressers it need not cost a fortune. In fact, there are many opportunities for you to advertise for free. Let's look at a few now.

Editorials

An editorial is a piece in the local paper that is written about a company, product or service from a 'news' perspective. This is to be distinguished from an 'advertorial'; a piece of advertising which is pretending to be editorial. Editorials are written by staff journalists, albeit from a press release they have received from the company they are writing about!

The benefit of an editorial is that readers will be more likely to read it – and believe it. Whereas an advert is always viewed will a slight air of scepticism – what are they trying to sell me? Your chances of getting editorial space depend on a number of factors: how much space the paper needs to fill in any given week, how interesting your 'angle' is, and whether the information is complete enough to be written up without any further research.

The first you can't do much about. If you decide to try and get editorial space in your local paper all you can do is write up your press release and hope for the best. But what is an angle, and how can you make one work for you?

An angle is something that is different, interesting or unique about you or your service. Or, preferably, all three! To qualify for an editorial, your story has to be NEWS. Maybe you have just completed a Master of Colour qualification. This is unusual enough to qualify as news if you were launching a new business. The question you must ask yourself is – can you see the headline?

The angle could be your own personal story, your own struggle for success, for example, or getting over an illness. Or it could be the type of service you are offering – the more unusual the better. Unusual would be specialising in children's hair; taking a box of toys around with you and having tiny gowns printed in bright colours. Or offering early

morning appointments to local business people (not for the faint-hearted, that one).

You get the picture. Write your press release, call the paper and ask who to send it to, send it and cross your fingers. If you are lucky, and it is a quiet week, you'll get a full page with photo (you'll need to send the photo as well, of course). If you are very unlucky you might get a few lines. Or nothing. But it will be free, so nothing ventured...

Paid-for advertising is easier – and can be costly. Small box ads in local papers cost from £30 a week upwards. Larger, full-colour ads can cost an arm and a leg. Are they worth it? This is an issue many hairdressers disagree on. Some say it is all about image and branding, others claim you only need to get your number out there and clients will call if they need you. To make your own decision you will have to go back to your planning and look closely at your target market. What kind of advertising will they respond to? And where will they be looking? Why?

Make a list of all the places you would like to advertise and then call the publications and get prices. Also consider their circulation – the village newsletter may be very cheap, but how many people actually read it?

Advertise in Local Newsletters

Local newsletters are a good way of targeting particular customers. An example of this is the newsletter published by the National Childbirth Trust (NCT). Distributed to its members quarterly, it sells advertising at a very reasonable rate. If your target market includes parents of young children within a middle-income bracket, this will bring your details right into the houses of those mums and dads.

Yellow pages

The Yellow Pages do make a charge for advertising, but this is undoubtedly the most used directory in the UK. Many potential clients will look in the Yellow Pages, or visit www. yell.com, to find details of local service, including hairdress- ing. A one line listing is free, and should prove well worth the effort. The only downside is if your details change within the year – the Yellow Pages will not be able to reflect this until the following years' directory comes out.

Local Area Websites

There are many online directories for regional areas – simply do a Google search yourself for local services and you will find some. Advertising with these is free, but may not pro- duce fantastic results – it will depend on how successful the site's own search engine status is.

On the Internet

Google's Adwords is a new way of advertising on the Inter- net, and it can be very cost-effective. The ads appear on the right hand side of Google's search results. The intricacies of Adsense are too complex to go into here (an easy to fol- low guide can be found at www.google.com/adsense), but basically you target your ad to reflect certain keywords, or search terms, such as hairdresser or haircut. Ads can also be targeted to only appear in certain locations. The really good thing about Adsense is that you pay only when some- body clicks on your ad, and you can set your own budget for each month, paying as little as £5.00 a month.

One obvious drawback is that you have to have at least a simple webpage for Adsense to work – when the ad is clicked on customers are directed to your webpage. How- ever, Google also provide free simple web pages

http://pages.google.com/-/about.html

that you can set up within minutes. The page needs only to have your prices, contact details and a little more information about you.

LEAFLETS

Leaflets are a popular method of gaining new business as they are cheap to design and produce, and can be targeted to one particular area, such as a certain housing estate or postcode. The take-up rate for leaflets is alarmingly low in general, so many will need to be distributed for any significant results in terms of new clients.

Designing a Leaflet – not just a price list

Many hairdressing leaflets are nothing other than price-lists with a phone number at the bottom. Printed on plain white, or perhaps yellow, paper. Dull, dull, dull. How many bits of paper do you get through your door in any given week? Do you read them all or do they go straight in the bin? Along with endless takeaway menus, leafleting seems to be popular for window cleaners, double glazing, garage door companies, cleaners and all manner of other small local businesses.

This kind of advertising is purely speculative. You put your leaflet through the door and hope that someone in that household might be thinking of having a haircut sometime soon. (Most people won't bother to hold on to leaflets for long.) You also hope that they are dissatisfied with their current hairdresser, or simply between hairdressers at the moment. And that they will get around to calling – before they lose the leaflet.

Okay, maybe this is too extreme a picture. Just don't expect too much from your leaflets, that's all. One way you can

improve your chances is by following a few advertising guidelines to make your leaflet stand out from the crowd.

Follow the AIDA principle: First, grab their Attention with an eye-catching headline, great photos or graphics. Next, pique their Interest with an intriguing fact or a question. Then you must create a Desire for your service by focussing on the benefits to the client – how much better they will look and feel after having their hair done by you, for example. Lastly, you need a call to Action – something to make them call you NOW, not next week. This can be a time-sensitive offer, such as a discount that only runs until a certain date, or a special offer for the first ten customers who book an appointment.

By all means include a sample of your prices if you wish, on the back of the leaflet if costs allow. But offer your potential customers something more if you want your bit of paper to stand out from all the rest.

Where and how to drop

The simplest, and cheapest, way to deliver (or drop) your leaflets is by doing it yourself. Pick a street that is in your target area, drive there, park up, and get walking. In the early days when business is thin this can be quite an enjoyable way to spend your down time – especially if you start your business in the summer! You don't have to feel guilty for being outside getting a tan as you are actually working on your business at the same time...

When business picks up, or if for other reasons you cannot do the leaflet drops yourself, you'll need to find someone else to do it for you. Unless you can persuade your younger brother or sister to do it for you, you'll probably have to pay. There are many companies who offer leafleting services. One of these is the Royal Mail, who will deliver leaflets to a particular postcode along with the mail. Prices are steep,

however, and considering the likely returns for the average mobile hairdresser, probably not worth considering.

Another option is to have your leaflets delivered along with your area's local newspaper. Costs for this will be far more reasonable, and leaflets that arrive in a person's house in this way don't tend to make it to the dustbin quite so quickly. Contact your local paper's advertising department to find out more.

One last option is to take a look at some of the bits of paper that land through your own door (assuming you live in your own target area, of course), and consider teaming up with another business, sharing the effort. This could either be a complimentary business, such as a nail technician or beauty therapist, or a non-complimentary business such as your local Chinese takeaway. It doesn't really matter as long as your leaflets are getting under the noses of your potential clients.

TALKS AND DEMONSTRATIONS

One marketing technique few hairdressers think of is giving talks and demonstrations, which is surprising as most hairdressers are fairly outgoing and all are very skilled. This method is used a lot by companies who sell products through trade or craft fairs, and can be very, very successful.

There are two ways of organising a demonstration: either by arranging it yourself or by going along as a guest speaker to another organisations event. The Women's Institute (WI) are always on the lookout for speakers on any topic, and although they do not pay this is a perfect opportunity to hand out cards, make contacts, and generally impress potential clients with your expert knowledge and experience.

If the WI is not your target market look around locally for other events. What about wedding fairs? Could you give a demonstration of a hair-up for brides and bridesmaids? You would need to book a stand or some space, and take along a few models (friends) and clips, pins, brushes etc. And a huge stack of business cards. (Don't forget your diary – you'll probably get booked up for the entire summer if your demonstration is any good!)

Local companies may be interested in having you in to give talks to their staff. The talk can be on anything hair-related; the importance of hair in first impressions, how good grooming increases confidence, how to style your hair in five minutes and look great. These are just a few ideas – the potential list is endless.

The other alternative is to organise an event yourself. You would need to hire out an appropriate venue, such as a community centre or rooms in a conference centre, and take care of the advertising, marketing and promotion. But if the title and content is likely to be very popular there is nothing to stop you charging for tickets. If this seems too big to manage alone, why not team up with a couple of complementary businesses and ask them to get involved?

Party Evenings
Another marketing tool often overlooked by hairdressers is the rise in party-selling. No longer confined to the likes of Tupperware, the party is a great way to get clients together in a fun, non-threatening atmosphere and gain new businesses.

Ask an existing client (someone who has a lot of contacts and a fairly big house is perfect), to invite some friends over for a hairdressing party. At the event you could start off with a short talk, introduce some products you have for sale, and

then give a cutting demo on your client. (This would be for free – her bonus for hosting the party.)

After a few glasses of wine (the clients, not you), you merely whip out your diary and take the bookings. An enjoyable evening that should gain you at least one new client, if not more.

POSTERS AND SPECIAL OFFERS

In our exhaustive list of marketing ploys, we will next take a look at the uses of posters and special offers. These are techniques which, if used wisely, can give your business an all-important boost at quiet times, and keep those new clients dribbling in just when you need them.

Designing Posters

Posters are different to leaflets in a number of ways – they should be bigger, for one thing, and even more eye-catching. The purpose of a poster is to grab the attention – not necessarily to provide a lot of information. The interest should be piqued, and it must be made very easy for potential clients to get hold of you should they wish to find out more.

One way of doing this is to design the poster to have a number of tear-off strips along the bottom, each printed with your phone number. This is, however, a lot more costly in terms of printing.

> **Consider this:** In the era of the mobile phone, this may not be too much of a worry, anyway. People can simply key your details into their phone and call you later. If they remember. It is up to you to design the poster so that they just have to call you RIGHT NOW! Refer back to the AIDA principles to refresh your memory on how this is achieved.

Where to Place Them
Now you have your wonderful, brightly coloured, well-designed poster, where should you put it?

Places of work – friends and family
The first place to consider is on the notice-boards of other businesses. Many of these are located in staff rooms and rest rooms – places where the staff are sitting, often bored, marking time until they have to return to their desks. If you create an interesting poster and they look at it often enough, it will be a simple matter of a phone call the next time they are looking for a new style.

Start with the places of work of your family and friends. All of them. Even the men, even those who work in the most unlikely of places. The important thing is to get the name of your company out there. This is free advertising (apart from the cost of the posters, of course), so this isn't the time to be picky or focus too heavily on your target market. Hand out the posters to all your friends, and don't forget to ask them if the poster has gone up yet. There is nothing wrong with a little gentle pressure.

Local shops and businesses
Your next step should be to try and get your poster displayed in other local shops and businesses. This can either be in their staff-only areas, such as staff-rooms, or for viewing by their customers as well – both would be ideal. If you have no contact at the business where you'd like to display a poster, consider offering a small discount to their staff in return. This could be especially useful if you really feel you would gain a good number of new clients by advertising there.

Information boards
Many shops and supermarkets have information boards for

their customers, and these are another great place to pin up your poster – if your target market will see it. Always keep in mind that you are trying to attract the right kind of customers – and lots of them – rather than just any old person.

> **_Consider this:_** Why does it matter, in the early days, whose hair you do? Because you are only one person and you need to spend your best resource – your time – wisely. Driving all over town spending time on clients who will never call you again because you aren't really what they are looking for is a waste of time. You should be focussing your efforts on your 'A' clients. In the following chapter we will look at what this means and how to do it.

Special Offers

There are many reasons and opportunities for having special offers. Here are some examples:

• In quieter times, such as January, you could run a special offer such as half-price colours when booked with a cut and blow-dry. This wouldn't eat into your costs too badly, but would encourage clients who are a little strapped for cash to book that appointment now rather than waiting.

• To gain new clients quickly, offer two-for-one on haircuts for existing clients and a friend, when another appointment is booked for the friend. This way, they get a half-price haircut each, but you get a guaranteed new client – and look very generous.

• If you have attended a training course, on a new colour technique for example, or hair-extensions, you could offer a limited-period discount on the new service. This is an excellent way of recouping training costs and introducing your clients to your new skills.

- When hairdressing wholesalers have VAT-free days or sales, go along and stock up on hair products to sell on to your clients. You could pass on a discount to your clients, making a lightly smaller profit yourself. The longer-term benefit of this, however, is that once your clients are using the products and like them, they will want to buy more from you – at the usual price.

These are just four examples of how special offers can help to grow your business. Using your own imagination you will no doubt be able to think of lots more.

Time Limits

When putting on a special offer, it is worth considering adding a time-limit. Not only does this give you a 'way out' of the offer if it proves too popular and starts to cost you money, it also creates a sense of urgency for your clients. Consider the following two examples of a hairdressing special offer:

**Perm Sale! 50% off perms.
Call to book an appointment.**

**Perm Sale! 50% off all perms booked
before the end of February.
Don't miss out! Call NOW to book
your appointment.**

Which of these examples would make you have your perm done sooner rather than later? Adding a time factor is the smart way of maximising the benefits of running a special offer.

Careful Wording

Just one more thing to consider before we move on to Discounts (and this applies to discount offers as well); word

your offers carefully. If the above offer only applied to the perm part of a perm, cut and blow dry, for example, you should say so. The difference could work out to be a considerable amount of money for you:

1 perm @ £20.00 + cut and blow dry @ £20
= £40 – your normal price

1 perm @ 50% off = £10 + cut and blow dry @ £20
= £30 – your offer price

1 perm, cut and blow dry @ 50% off
= £20 – NOT your offer price, but £10 less!

Consider also the wording where the time-sensitive factor is concerned. If the offer is available only during the month of February, does this mean appointments booked in February for any time in the coming weeks, or only appointments actually taken in February?

If your offer only applies after a minimum spend, say so. If it only applies to ladies' cut and blow drys, and not men's, say so. Make sure your offer is pretty water tight to discourage wily clients taking advantage – and you ending up out of pocket.

DISCOUNTS

To a certain degree, we have covered elements of discounts while looking at Special Offers. But there are other types of discounts you can use to increase your business, and these are ones which are offered as a permanent incentive, not just a one-time only offer.

Why Offer a Discount?

Discounts can be used to access a large group of people and gain clients in greater numbers than would otherwise be

possible. They can create loyalty and engender many refer-rals. A discount, offered exclusively, can give a potential cli-ent the incentive to change from their existing hairdresser to you. It is not necessarily about saving money – an important point to remember.

The discount doesn't have to be huge, and it isn't to imply that the client can't afford your services. (You don't want cli-ents who can't afford you – they aren't part of your target market.) Offering a permanent discount is a way of saying 'Your business is important to me and I would like to have you as one of my clients'. That's all.

Local Businesses
One very successful area to access with discounts are large local business, such as head offices for banks, manufactur-ing, large chains, department stores – anywhere that has a lots of staff who fit your target market in the main (there may be a few who don't but we are talking numbers here so it doesn't matter too much).

Contact the Human Resources department of the company and tell them you would like to offer a discount on hairdress-ing services for their staff. Tell them how much that discount will be. (10% is a nice round figure.) Offer to send them some leaflets, price lists, business cards and posters, and ask if they will let their staff know.

It really is as simple as that. Your poster will be displayed in staff rooms (with details of the discount clearly explained), and the staff of the company will probably be told about the offer in newsletters or circular emails. Many local businesses do this and it is an excellent way of growing your client list – with minimum effort from you.

The only reason a company might say "No, thank you", is if

they are already using a discount from another hairdresser. If that is the case, make a note and call again every six months or so to see if the situation has changed. Move on to your next company.

TIP: *Make sure you let the company's staff know to quote a reference when they call to book an appointment (this can simply be the company's name). That way you know which discount to apply, and can keep track of which marketing threads are working. (More on this later in Keeping Track Of What Works.)*

Free Advertising
Another reason for promoting your business in this way is for the advertising gained by having your business name displayed on yet more posters and leaflets in even more places. This is part of creating a brand, and the better your brand, or image, the higher prices you can charge and the better quality of clients you will attract.

WEBSITES

More and more mobile hairdressers are going online and developing a web presence, following in the footsteps of salons and other professional services. These websites can be as simple as what is known as a 'business card' site, where just your contact details, and perhaps a few prices and photos, are shown, or as complex as an interactive site where clients can book appointments in real time, or buy hair products by mail-order.

Why Have a Website
If everybody else is doing it then so should you! This is not the only reason, but it is a good one. Here are a few more good reasons for having your own website:

Professional image

If your target market and business model warrants it, then the professional appearance given to a business by having its own website can't be underestimated – IF it is a really nice website. Having a site that is annoyingly slow, or irritatingly fussy and complicated will not improve your professional appearance at all. However, a website that has a clean, stylish look and feel, with a few carefully chosen images and easy-to-read text will raise your profile way above the competition.

Shop front

In many ways a website is even more important for a mobile hairdressing business than for a salon, as it is your only shop-front – albeit a virtual one. Being a mobile business, the only other opportunity you have for displaying your phone number and business name is on the side of your car! With a website you can design an image that fits your business, and show it to the world.

Your website is often the first place a potential client will go to find out about what kind of business you are. If you display your web address (or URL) on all your advertising, many people will visit the website before calling to book an appointment. If it appeals to them, and looks like the kind of salon they would like to go to, they will call. If it doesn't, chances are they won't. So if you have a website, make sure it says all the right things about you and your business.

Easy to find

Having a website can make you easier for clients to find. If they know your business name, for example, but have forgotten your phone number, they can Google you and there you are. Remember Google Adwords? If you don't have a website you won't be able to take advantage of this excellent

way of advertising. Online directories, for your local area, will offer free listings and a link to take potential customers directly to your website.

Important information

As well as your contact details, your website can tell clients all sorts of important information, such as your trading hours, how to leave or send a message, your prices and availability. The website can include a contact form so they can easily send an enquiry, along with photos of hairstyles, any news-clippings about you, a brief CV or resume – anything, in fact, that you feel would appeal to your target clients and improve the chances that they will call you and book an appointment.

TIP: *On your website you could include a map of the area, or areas you cover. This is an easy way for clients to see if it is worth calling, and saves you time answering enquiries from clients who are out of your region.*

Keeping up with emails when you're on the road

The only problem with having a web presence is that it will increase the number of emails you receive – emails that need to be answered. This isn't a problem for businesses that are office based; with a computer in front of you all day answering an email is easier than making a phone call. For that reason, many clients will expect their email enquiries to be answered very promptly – and not be too impressed if they are not.

As a mobile hairdresser, you will probably find it hard enough to keep up with the phone messages that you come home to every night, let alone emails! Don't these people under-stand that you are driving around all day? There is no easy answer to this problem other than to try very hard to keep on top of things.

One idea is to include a message on your website which gently and politely reminds clients that you are out on the road a lot, and tells them how quickly you intend to answer their enquiry – within 48 hours, for example. Then set aside a particular time of day when you will go to your computer and check – and answer – your emails. This could be first thing in the morning while you're having your breakfast, or last thing at night. It doesn't matter as long as you do it regularly.

Professional Design or Create Your Own?

Now you have decided to have a website, should you hire someone to do it for you or create one yourself? It is certainly a lot easier and less time consuming to pay someone else, but web design is a costly business and you may find your budget is a little stretched to begin with. For what you will need the site to do, it probably won't be worth spending a fortune on a website. You can always upgrade to a more sophisticated site later in your career if your business needs it.

Remember we talked about Domain Names earlier? Hopefully you chose a business name that was available as a URL, and possibly even bought that URL ready for your website. If not, you can find web hosting companies who offer domain registration along with basic site templates that are ready and waiting for you to add your own information to.

A template-site is the perfect solution for a simple 'business card' website. The hosting service, such as 1&1 or MrSite, will provide you with an easy to follow process for adding your own contact details, pictures, and other content. Most offer email facilities, online contact forms, and a wide choice of colours and style. Some even offer blogs, simple shopping carts, and all sorts of other features.

Expect to pay in the region of £5 per month for hosting of a simple template site, and a further £20 per two years for domain registration. (Correct at the time of writing.)

 how2become

KEEPING TRACK OF WHAT WORKS

The last area to think about when building your business is keeping track of your marketing endeavours. You are spending a lot of time – and possible money – on promoting your business, and (if you are doing it right) calls are coming in all the time from new clients. Well done! You are building a successful business.

Now for a few questions (Yes, this is a test):

• Which of your posters pulled in the most clients last month?

• Which area leafleted produced the best results? What percentage of leaflets to clients was that?

• How many clients came from discounted or special offers?

• How much money did that make you? (And were those offers worthwhile?)

• How many clients have you gained via referrals?

• How much money did they spend with you, and have they been back again?

• Which of your existing clients have referred the most?

• How many hits has your website had so far?

• How many clients have found you via the internet?

• Which marketing stream, all in all, is your most successful to date?

If you couldn't answer all of these questions (with a little time to look through your records), you aren't taking care of the most IMPORTANT part of all marketing – Keeping Track Of What Works (And What Doesn't Work)!

Some Promotions are More Successful Than Others

If this is your first time in business, and if you haven't had much to do with marketing before, running promotions is a bit like scrambling about in the dark. You think of an idea. You run it past your partner or best friend. You ask a couple of clients what they think. (This is the extent of most people's market research!)

You decide to run with it, so you print off a few posters or leaflets, distribute them, and then get on with your work. Occasionally clients mention where they heard about you, and you nod politely, but you're just grateful for the work, really.

There is nothing wrong with being busy. But you are making a grave mistake if you forget to take notice of where your clients are coming from. While some promotions are naturally going to be more successful than others, when you get around to running them again, how are you going to know which promotions to run?

Take advertising – one of the biggest costs for mobile hairdressers after fuel. You have probably advertised in a number of places, with some of your adverts more expensive than others. It is easy to keep on placing ads and paying for advertising with a publication that is actually not bringing you any business at all! At the same time, you may let an advert lapse in a place which has been responsible for bringing you over 50% of your new clients so far.

The point is – you need to know where your clients are coming from. That way you can make informed choices about your marketing as time goes on and you learn what works and what doesn't . And the way to find out where they came from? Ask them.

Have a system of always asking new clients how they found out about you, and make a note of this in your diary, along with their name, address and phone number. Then, at the end of the week when you do your accounts (what do you mean, you don't do them every week?), you can add the information on marketing to a simple spreadsheet (see below) which will help you to build a picture of what is working – and what isn't.

A Simple Chart

Below is an example of a simple way of keeping track of all your marketing:

Marketing Spreadsheet for July

TYPE OF ADVERT/ PROMOTION	WHERE PLACED	COST	# OF CLIENTS	SALES GAINED	COST/ CLIENT
Box ad: 1 x 2 inches	Local paper	£45/month	5	£100	£9
Poster	Co-op	£5	0	0	£5
Colouring sale: 50% off colours	Leaflets to clients and word of mouth	Reduction in profits	10	£300	£10
Half page colour advert	Local link magazine	£80	2	£30	£40

By keeping track of your marketing threads, it is easy to see at a glance what is making you money – and what is a complete waste of time. In the above example, the colouring sale was by far the most profitable venture of the month – netting £200 in profit. (£300 sales, minus £10 costs for 10 clients.) These were existing clients, however, who may have had the colour done anyway.

The second most successful was the box ad in the local paper. This brought in 5 brand new clients, at a cost of only £9 per client, netting £55 profit in total. If this continues to be as successful this would be a valuable drip of new clients, for very little outlay. If, however, the rate of new clients drops off, it would be worth considering whether £45 a month is too high a spend.

The poster in the Co-op didn't do well this month, but it does only cost £5. If its performance doesn't improve it could be cut, and the £5 spent elsewhere. The half page colour advert in the local link magazine should be dropped immediately, however. It cost more per client than if you gained in total sales for both of those clients – not a good use of your resources.

Which just goes to show – it isn't always the adverts you like best, or which look the prettiest, that bring in the clients.

Whether you devise your own way of keeping track of your marketing, or use a chart like the one above, make sure you always know what is working for you and what isn't. Then, if business starts to slacken and you need to inject some life back into it, you will instantly know where to go.

CHAPTER FOUR
YOUR MOST IMPORTANT ASSET; CLIENTS

So far we have focussed on all the preliminary stuff of running a mobile hairdressing business; planning, marketing, building your business. Now it's time to focus on the really important stuff. You thought the last three chapters were the important stuff? Not as important as keeping your business afloat!

A huge percentage of new businesses go under in their first year. Over half of the rest fail within the next five years. Those aren't great odds. Of course, yours are much more favourable – you have read this book!

Still, it won't hurt to spend a little time thinking about how to keep your business going from strength to strength. And the way to do this is to always keep your focus on your number one asset: your clients.

CUSTOMER CARE

We have all had experiences of terrible customer care – or

'Customers? I don't care!' as some shops seem to be saying. When we receive bad service from a company we don't want to continue to deal with them – no matter how good their product might be.

Remember this important point: You might well be the best, most skilled hairdresser in the world, but if you don't look after your clients properly and treat them well, you will never be successful in business.

Conversely, even if you are an average hairdresser, with fairly good skills (but wouldn't win any competitions, perhaps), you can still build up a fantastically profitable business if you have the right attitude.

Your clients, quite simply, are your business. Ignore their needs at your peril.

Making clients feel special

The first thing to remember is that each and every one of your clients needs to be made to feel special. The time they have booked with you is their time, and their time alone. Try to limit the number of phone calls you take while you are with one client – if necessary, turn your phone off until you leave. If you absolutely have to answer the phone, apologise and keep the call short and to the point.

Don't talk non-stop about yourself. Of course your clients are interested in hearing all about you and what you have been up to since they saw you last. But they also want to feel that you are interested in them. Try to remember at least one thing about them – their children's names, their favourite restaurant, where they work, an event they are looking forward to.

If your memory isn't very good, make notes when you leave each client. A few words in your diary, referred to when you

next visit, could make the difference between client retention and client attrition.

Another way to make clients feel special is to listen and take them seriously when they talk about their hair. Yes, many clients are difficult to please, and yes, some do have unrealistic expectations. But your job, as their hairdresser, is to make them feel that they are easy to please, realistic, and a joy to work with. Manage this, and you will have the most loyal clients around.

Time management

You absolutely must not mess your clients around when it comes to their time. Time management is one of the most important skills of the mobile hairdresser – and one of the hardest to master when your clients are spread all over town, with bad traffic, school runs and speed-cameras all fighting against you.

The key is to allow enough time for appointments. Read this again. Allowing enough time for appointments reduces the chances of your running late, and causing your clients, and yourself, unnecessary stress. It will be tempting to pack your clients in tightly – you need to earn money and this may seem like a sensible strategy at first. You will soon come unstuck, as clients begin to get fed up with you always being late, always being rushed, always chasing your tail.

There is a far easier way – and it takes us back to planning, and our minimum hourly charge. Once you have worked out your initial figures and come up with your minimum hourly charge, you need only to make sure your prices reflect this and there is no need to pack in too many clients into too short a time-slot. It is usually hairdressers who are actually charging too little who end up over-booking in this way.

Other ways in which you can master time management and keep your clients happy:

• Know your area very, very well, so you can more accurately predict travelling times.

• Always allow yourself a lunch hour. If you begin to get behind, you can use this time to catch up.

• Write your clients' phone numbers in your diary, or carry your address book with you at all times, so you can at least call clients to let them know you will be late.

• Fill up with fuel on your way home each day. This way you won't be caught out, late and running on an empty tank.

Your clients are also busy people. They may have taken an afternoon off work to get their hair done, organised child-care, cancelled other appointments, etc. If you can't show them the respect to at least turn up on time, why would they keep having you back? No matter how good you think you are.

QUESTIONNAIRES

A great way to keep your clients happy is to find out what makes them happy. But this is easier said than done. If you ask your average client if they are happy with your service they will probably say yes. (It's a brave client who will say no when you have a pair of scissors in your hand!)

One way to find out is to give your clients a questionnaire they can fill in, anonymously if they prefer, giving you a clear picture of what you are doing right, what you're doing wrong, and what other services or changes your clients might appreciate.

Below is a sample questionnaire you could use, giving an idea of the kind of questions you might want to ask. Feel free to add your own questions and adapt the questionnaire to fit your own business.

Hair 2 U – Client Questionnaire

This questionnaire is designed to help me bring to you the best possible hairdressing service. It will also give me valuable information regarding your likes and dislikes, and help to shape the future of Hair 2 U.

You can either hand the completed questionnaire back to me today, or send it anonymously to the address below. Please be honest and frank; it is your views I am interested in.

SECTION A: **About You** *(this information will help to build a picture of my clients' lifestyles; please leave out any questions you do not wish to answer.)*

1. How long have you been using Hair 2 U?

☐ Less than 6 months
☐ 6 months to 1 year
☐ 1 to 5 years
☐ More than 5 years

2. How did you find out about Hair 2 U?

☐ Local press
☐ Recommended
☐ Leaflet/poster
☐ Other (please specify) _____

3. Are you employed outside the home?

☐ No
☐ Yes – please circle one: full time   part time   shift work

4. Your household consists of…

☐ Yourself
☐ Yourself & your partner
☐ You, your partner and children
☐ Other

SECTION B: **About Hair 2 U**

1. Why do you continue to use Hair 2 U?

(Please list the following reasons in order of importance from 1 through to 5, with 1 being the most important and 5 being the least. Please use all five numbers.)

____ Convenience

____ Price

____ Flexible appointment times

____ Person who cuts your hair

____ Feels comfortable

2. Please score the following aspects of the Hair 2 U service: (please tick)

	EXCELLENT	GOOD	OK	POOR
Reliability				
Value for money				
Availability of appointments				
Ease of booking appointments				
Professionalism				

Quality of hairdressing				
Listening to you/ meeting your needs				

3. If you were to consider using another hairdressing service, what would your main reason be?

☐ Price
☐ Convenience
☐ The 'Salon' experience
☐ Other_____

4. If you are unhappy with the hairdressing service you receive, please use this space to explain why.

_____
_____
_____
_____

SECTION C: **The Future**

What, if anything, could Hair 2 U do or change to make you happier with the service?

_____
_____
_____
_____
_____
_____

Thank you for taking the time to complete this question-naire. Your comments will be treated confidentially and are much appreciated.

NAME & ADDRESS (optional):

_____

_____

_____

_____

Case study:

Marcus had been running his mobile hairdressing business for about six years when he decided to give his clients the opportunity to feed back. He had noticed that a few clients had slipped away recently, and was starting to feel as though his business was a little stale.

Marcus handed out questionnaires and read the responses with trepidation. He was relieved at first – most of his clients rated his abilities very highly and showed their loyalty and commitment with their glowing comments.

With more careful reading, however, Marcus noticed a pattern emerging. While almost all of his clients said they were happy with his skills, many clearly weren't quite so happy with the service he offered. There were lots of comments about how hard he was to get hold of, how long he took to answer phone calls, and his general availability.

Marcus took his clients' comments seriously. He organised his time so he answered messages within 24 hours, and added two late evening slots a week. His business is now thriving.

NEWSLETTERS

Another great way of keeping your clients happy and making them feel special is to produce a regular newsletter. This doesn't have to be weekly (who has the time?), bi-monthly,

or even quarterly, is fine. Your newsletter can include an up-to-date price list, any news about training courses you have recently attended, and perhaps a brief piece of advice for a common hair-related problem.

Your newsletter needn't be an epic! One side of A4, printed on your own printer at home in black and white is perfectly sufficient. Clients will still be grateful you've taken the trouble to keep in contact with them in this way, and it will put you head and shoulders above the competition.

TIP: *Send your newsletter out to lapsed clients (see next section) as well. These are clients you haven't heard from for a while, and whose normal time between appointments has passed. They may have gone elsewhere, they may be simply 'growing' their hair, they may just be a bit short on cash. Sending them your latest newsletter reminds them who you are and might just be the nudge they need to call you again.*

Below is an example of the kind of newsletter you could send out to your clients:

ℌair 2U

Welcome! to the first Hair 2 U newsletter - spring/summer

✂ *Hair 2 U was established in July 2001, to bring a professional, salon-standard service to people in the comfort of their own homes. Thanks to you, and your support,* **Hair 2 U** *is going from strength to strength.*

✂ *In this issue: how to get the best out of your mobile hairdresser, booking your appointment.*

Please read the terms and conditions on the reverse of this newsletter, and find out how you are protected by a FULL GUARANTEE and insurance.

There will be a small price increase to take effect from 1st April. Please see below for details.

How to Get the Best out of your Mobile Hairdresser – Do's and Don'ts

DO provide the best possible environment within your home. The kitchen is usually best, with an easy to sweep floor, surfaces for your hairdresser's bags and equipment, and electricity sockets nearby. Ensure there is adequate lighting and have a suitable chair ready.

DO talk to your stylist about your hairstyle, and show her pictures if necessary, to ensure you both have the same hairstyle in mind.

DON'T forget to check your hair thoroughly before your stylist leaves.

DO try to minimize distractions and interruptions which may spoil your haircut. Your Hair 2 U experience should be as relaxing and enjoyable as possible.

DO ask for advice on styling and maintaining your hair.

DON'T be afraid to try new styles or experiment with a new colour or image. Your stylist will be happy to advise you.

Booking Your Appointment

I am aware that many clients find me difficult to get hold of as I work long hours and can't always answer my mobile phone – especially if I am driving!

Booking your appointment in advance is the best way to ensure you get the date and time you would like. Alternatively, call 00000 888888 and leave a detailed message and I will get back to you as soon as I can.

New Prices for Spring/Summer

Cut & blow dry...£20.00
Wet cut..£15.00
Blow dry £15.00
Full head tint inc. C&BD..£40.00
Full head tint, no cut £30.00
Cap hi-lights inc. C&BD (short hair)...........................£35.00
Cap hi-lights, no cut £30.00
Foil hi-lights inc. C&B..from £50.00
Foil hi-lights, no cut from £40.00
Tone-on-tone colour inc. C&BD £30.00
Tone-on-tone colour, no cut......................................£27.00
Perm inc. C&BD ....from £40.00
Gents (with ladies appointment only)...........................£8.00
Children (with ladies appointment only):
Up to 6 years..£3.00 - £5.00
6 to 10 years ....£5.00 - £8.00
10 to 14 years ....£8.00 - £10.00

Special Thanks to Sue, who received a FREE haircut in return for recommending 5 of her friends to Hair 2 U. Could you beat that?

Bearing in mind that your clients are your most important asset, you must get into the habit of doing everything within your power to retain their business. How will you know if you are losing clients? You need to keep some kind of database so you can review it regularly and see who is currently booking appointments and who has fallen by the wayside.

A simple spreadsheet is all that is needed. Have columns with the names and addresses of your clients, when they booked their last appointment, and when their next is due. This may be anything from one to eight weeks, depending on the client and the service they usually have.

Once a week update the spreadsheet from the information in your diary, and then look at the dates for your 'overdue' clients. Once these clients become more than a month overdue, they should be considered 'lapsed', and their details entered into another spreadsheet or list.

Never forget about your lapsed clients. They are far more valuable to you than you realise. Getting them back may be a lot cheaper than getting new clients to replace them with, through costly advertising or promotions. Your lapses clients have tried you out, they know you, and they know (hopefully) that you are professional and skilled. Whatever their reasons for straying, there is every chance you could win them back.

Try the following tips:

• Send a reminder card after a few weeks – your client may well have only lost your number

• Send another reminder card if you haven't heard anything for another month

• Send out your newsletter to lapsed clients as well as current ones

• Run a promotion at least four times a year and include your lapsed clients in your mail-shots

• Never stop sending them information – until they call and ask you to!

Consequences of losing clients

Remember that old saying; If your business isn't growing it is shrinking? That is the consequence of losing clients. Your client base is everything. It is your entire business's worth. If you have 100 clients on your books, each having their hair done roughly 8 times a year, and spending on average £30 each, you have sales of £24,000 a year. This, minus your costs, is your income.

If you lose only 5% of those clients over the course of a year, your sales drop to £22800 – a loss of £1200! That is a lot of money. And it doesn't take much to lose 5% of your clientele – that is only 5 clients. Think about it. Are there 5 clients you haven't heard from in a while? Or more, even? This is costing you money. Try everything in your power to get them back, and at the same time continue your marketing efforts to get more – just in case...

How to lose clients

Now for a master-class in how to lose clients:

Number One: Don't listen

Top of the list, as it is the main reason given by people when asked why they gave up on their old hairdresser. Hairdressers who don't listen to their clients are asking to be abandoned! Common complaints are: cut too much off when I asked for a trim; my hair looked nothing like the picture; always turns out the same no matter what I ask for.

There is no excuse for this. Your clients' hair is just that – your clients' hair. Not yours. It is up to them how they want to look for the next six weeks, so LISTEN!

Number Two: Don't turn up

A fairly obvious one this, but it is surprising how many

hairdressers book appointments and then don't bother to turn up. An excuse, and hopefully an apology, may follow, but the damage is already done. In this day and age of mobile technology, there really is no reason for not letting a client know if you can't make their appointment.

Number Three: Never be on time

We covered this at length in Time Management, but it is worth revisiting. Clients will forgive you a lot, and a being late a few times is no problem, especially if you apologise and give a genuine reason. But continue to be late, and then rush their hair when you get there, and your clients will drop you faster than a hot potato.

Number Four: Don't give them value for money

Notice that this doesn't read – Charge too much. There is a difference. Many clients are happy to pay a lot – a LOT – for their haircuts, but few are willing to be ripped off. Liken this to a top restaurant – if you are paying £50 a head and are promised fine dining, you won't be impressed with basic pub grub. Hairdressing is no different. Charge your clients top prices by all means, but make sure your skills and service are up to the job.

Number Five: Be full of yourself and intimidating

Okay, I know you don't mean to be. But hairdressers can be, you know. A little. At least, this is another complaint by many disgruntled clients. Dressing too outrageously, talking in too much graphic detail about your exploits at the weekend, appearing to look down your nose at clients, all these things are guaranteed to upset and alienate your clients.

So now you know. Avoid the above like the plague and you shouldn't go too wrong. If you can master keeping your

clients happy, getting their thoughts and feedback, and offering an exceptional service, you should never need to worry about losing clients again.

FOLLOW-UP SERVICES

Running a successful mobile hairdressing business is not just about visiting your clients and doing their hair. There are many extras you can give to your clients –this section is all about added-value.

Sending reminder cards

We briefly mentioned reminder cards when looking at how to tempt back lapsed clients; let's look at these in a little more detail.

A reminder card is a gentle reminder that your client has gone beyond the period of time that usually elapses between their appointments. It should be worded very carefully so it doesn't seem in any way bullying – you don't want to be likened to the dentist!

Sending a card, however, is a professional and courteous thing to do for your clients, who may have genuinely forgotten their hair cut is due, or lost your number, or just been too busy. Many clients will receive your card with gratitude, and call the very next day.

Below is an example of a reminder card, which could be printed four to an A4 sheet and sent out by second class post to save costs:

Hair 2 U

[Your contact details here]

Dear [insert client's name]

Just a note to remind you that it is approximately six weeks since your last appointment with Hair 2 U.

I hope you were happy with your hair;

please call [your number here] for another appointment.

If you don't receive a response from this reminder card, it may be worth sending out another, with the following wording:

Just a note to let you know that it has been a while since your last appointment with Hair 2 U.

As a valued customer, I'd love to hear from you. Please call [your number here] for an appointment.

If after these two reminders you still haven't heard from the clients in question, add them to your lapsed list and begin your campaign to win them back!

Keeping a database
A lot of the above advice relies on your keeping an up-to-date database of your clients and all their relevant information. Of course, your database doesn't have to be an actual database, with complicated fields and search queries. Your client database can be as simple as your own hand-written notes in an exercise book. Many mobile hairdressers keep their clients' details on a simple spreadsheet, in a programme like Excel on their home computer.

The information you will need to keep includes: name and addresses, telephone numbers, details of colours/perms/products that your client uses, dates of their last appointments, details of any correspondence (such as reminder cards or letters), and anything else you feel is relevant.

The important thing about a database is to keep it up to date. This means taking time, at least once a week, to add information and check dates etc. Your database will be a valuable tool in managing your most important asset, so give it as much attention as you can.

The Data Protection Act – what you need to know
If you keep your information about your clients on computer, you need to comply with the Data Protection Act. Ignorance of the Act is not a defence against failure to comply, so be sure to familiarise yourself with the guidelines and keep on the right side of the law.

GIVING ADVICE

While we are on the subject of keeping clients happy, it is worth considering a few extra services which you could offer to your clients, and potential clients, which will set you apart from other mobile hairdressers and give you that all-important edge.

Have you ever noticed how whenever you meet someone new, the minute they find out you are a hairdresser they ask, *'What would you do with my hair?'* You then spend the rest of the night giving them free advice! Maybe they are seriously considering using your services, maybe they aren't...

But why not use this skill to improve even further your standing with clients. It costs you nothing (except time, which we will come to in a moment) to visit someone and take a quick

look at their hair. This is especially useful with new clients who are thinking of having a colour – if you've never met them how can you possibly know which colours to take?

Follow-up advice

Free advice can also be a useful follow-up service for clients who might be having trouble keeping their hair looking as fantastic as it did when you left them. Often it is easy for you to spot the problem immediately (using the wrong brush, not finishing their hair off properly, incorrect application of product), and requires little effort from you. To your client, however you will have performed a small miracle!

After a colour or perm

Any treatment which chemically alters the structure of the hair needs careful aftercare, something which clients don't always manage too well on their own. Offering any kind of follow-up after a colour or a perm will do two important things: It will make you extremely popular with your clients, and it will ensure their hair looks great all the time, thus winning them more compliments and you more referrals.

A follow-up doesn't have to be in the form of a visit, however, if your time is very limited. You could simply produce a useful leaflet to hand out to clients after a treatment, with detailed advice on how to wash, dry, style and care for their new look. Another idea is to ensure they can buy all they need to look after their hair from you at the time of your visit – shampoo, conditioner, styling products, brushes. This is the way to offer a complete service to your clients – the way successful salons do.

Visiting clients for advice or consultations – is it worth your time?

Obviously your time is extremely valuable. It is the one resource you can't afford to waste. So does visiting clients

in situations when there is no immediate payment count as a waste of that time?

Not necessarily. It helps to take a longer view. If a new client needs a little encouragement first, needs to see you are serious and professional and willing to go the extra mile, why not give them that? They could turn out to be your most profitable client. Or, you might never hear from them again. It is a risk, but a worthwhile one.

Once you know your area well, you will probably be able to squeeze in these 'free' visits between other clients, when you are in the vicinity. It certainly wouldn't be wise to travel a great distance just to look at a new client's hair (not with the price of fuel the way it is).

DEALING WITH COMPLAINTS

Complaints are a fact of life when your business involves other people. And how you deal with complaints will make the difference between happy clients – and a successful business – and angry, disappointed clients. Dealing well in the face of a complaint is an art form, and one which, sadly, not all hairdressers are taught as part of their training. If you find complaints very difficult to cope with, and tend to shy away from dealing with them, study the following advice very carefully:

1. Firstly, don't ever take a complaint personally. The client is complaining about their hair – not you. You are not their hair. Remember this – it will affect your response and the eventual outcome. Your clients may say: 'You have messed up my hair'. You need to be hearing: 'My hair is messed up. Help me'.

2. Once your own ego is out of the way, listen very

carefully to your client. This is mainly so your client feels listened to. You may have got the gist of their complaint within a few seconds and be eager to get on with the job of rectifying it. But the client still needs to feel listened to. She has probably been planning what to say for hours – or even days. Give her a chance to get it out so she feels better.

3. Stay very calm. If your client is angry (which doesn't happen often but it can happen), this is hard. Practice taking deep breaths and saying to yourself 'She is only angry because her hair is important to her confidence'. If you don't fuel her anger it will calm very quickly. Then you can get on with solving her problem.

4. Never disagree with a client. Even if you can plainly see that they are wrong, or if you know for a fact that the problem is one of their own making, like washing their hair the minute your back was turned after a perm, instead of waiting for 48 hours like you recommended! There are subtle ways to remind a client of their responsibilities later, once the complaint has been dealt with.

5. Always rectify the problem for free, and as soon as you reasonably can. It is not reasonable for a client to expect you to make a visit to them at 10.00pm on a Friday night because they have just discovered their fringe is still a bit long. It is reasonable for a client to expect you to make an effort to correct a mistake within 24 hours if they call at a reasonable time on a working day – especially if they have an important function to attend.

6. Thank your client for giving you the opportunity to put their hair right. Yes, thank them. Even if they got angry. Even if you disagree with their complaint. Try to put yourself in their shoes – it is hard to complain, and they

were probably very anxious about it and are hoping you don't feel bad about them. If you thank them for bringing the problem to your attention, your client will be so grateful they will be with you for life.

DIFFICULT SITUATIONS

As a mobile hairdresser, there will be times where you find yourself in difficult situations. Hopefully these will be few and far between, but when they do happen it pays to be prepared.

When something goes wrong

One type of difficult situation which you may come up against is if something goes wrong while you are doing a client's hair. If a colour, perm or other treatment goes wrong (which can happen, no matter how careful you are), as a mobile hairdresser you are completely on your own. If you worked in a salon, there may be a more senior member of staff you could turn to for help and support, or at the very least a colleague to bounce ideas off.

The moment you realise a service has gone wrong your heart sinks and panic sets in. What are you going to do? Will the client notice? (They will.) How can you put it right? Do you even have the products with you to put it right? (This will be the one time you have left them at home.)

First of all, don't panic. And don't try to cover up the problem. In the unlikely event that a treatment goes wrong, stay calm and try to assess the situation objectively. Make a mental note of what the solution is, and then explain it to your client. This will be hard, but if you are telling them the solution as well as the problem, in a calm and capable way, your client won't be too distressed.

Advice and support

If you are a member of a professional organisation such as the FHBF, you will have access to a helpline for situations like these. This can be invaluable when you are out and about on your own. Keep their number on you and don't be afraid to excuse yourself from your client for a moment to give the advice line a call.

Other hairdressers can be a valuable source of support, also. There is nothing to stop a group of mobile hairdressers getting together regularly to share stories and advice. Providing you can promise to leave each other's clients alone, of course. Or maybe you could stay in touch with colleagues from a salon you have worked in. Don't burn your bridges – there might come a time when you need a little advice and help.

Companies who manufacture products often have help lines for support with using the products. The larger companies like Wella and L'Oreal offer excellent support to hairdressers, as well as advice should anything go wrong. For colours, many shade charts have handy reference guides on mixing and colour corrections.

If all else fails, try calling your local hairdressing college. College lecturers have seen it all in their training salons and are often experts at rectifying (sometimes quite serious) mistakes. They would no doubt be happy to offer free advice in return for you giving their students a talk on running a mobile business.

Case study:
Freda had coloured Mrs Dean's hair before but she had always used a high-lifting tint – very successfully. Then one day, during a visit for a haircut only, Mrs Dean decided she would like to go lighter, and asked Freda to pop in a few

bleach hi-lights.

Freda says: "I didn't really have a lot of time, and with hind-sight I should have said no. But Mrs Dean was insistent and I hated to disappoint her." Freda only had 40 volume peroxide in her supplies bag that day, for use with another client later.

"I don't know why I did it, but I just thought it would help the bleach to lift more quickly, saving me time. I mixed the bleach with the 40 vol, weaved a few foils and left Mrs Dean's hair to develop while I gave her daughter a quick trim."

Distracted, Freda didn't realise something was wrong until it was too late. "Mrs Dean started to complain that her head felt hot and burny. I rushed to check her hair – and the bleach had swollen in the meche pockets and was burning her scalp."

That was nothing compared to what the chemical had done to Mrs Dean's hair. Where the product had been applied the hair was breaking away a couple of centimetres from the roots.

"I felt terrible," Freda says. "Because I had been in a hurry I had mixed the bleach up too strong, and hadn't allowed for the temperature of the room in the development time. I guess I had no way of knowing that Mrs Dean's hair would be so sensitive to bleach – but I should have been checking."

Thankfully, Freda had only put a few hi-lights in her client's hair, so the damage wasn't too visible. Mrs Dean is still using her services – but is a little reticent to have hi-lights again!

Threatening situations

Thankfully, few mobile hairdressers find themselves in threat-ening situations, but it is worth a mention as it does happen occasionally. A threatening situation is one where you feel uncomfortable, for whatever reason. This may be due to the

area you are visiting, if there are gangs hanging around, for example, or because of a specific client or their situation.

Visiting clients in their own homes means that you are exposed to their lives, in a way you never would be in a salon. You will meet their family, their friends, see their visitors, and hear all about their various problems. Occasionally this can bring you into contact with situations that involve drugs, certain types of crime, or anything else that you would rather avoid.

If you find yourself in such a situation, aim to leave as soon as is possible without drawing too much attention to yourself. If the situation around you is one you are uncomfortable with, but you are not the focus of the threat, finish your work quietly, collect payment (if it is forthcoming), then leave. Don't go back.

If you are the focus of the threats, leave immediately. Always carry your mobile phone and call the police if you have to. Remember the earlier advice about not carrying too much cash around with you. Make yourself the least likely target possible – avoiding threatening situations is the easiest way of dealing with them.

In the unlikely event of a client refusing to pay, and becoming aggressive if you insist, leave their home and then write a letter asking for payment. Sometimes a client will reconsider their behaviour later and send payment, along with an apology. More likely, however, is that you will never hear from them again – and good riddance!

COMMON PROBLEMS AND HOW TO RECTIFY THEM

If you are losing clients, or simply finding that your sales are slipping, there are a number of reasons why this might be.

Re-read the section on How To Lose Clients and check that you are doing everything in your power to keep your clients happy. For other situations, check the list below for common problems and their solutions.

Missed appointments
If a client isn't there when you turn up, you have two options: wait for a while and see if they show, or put a note through the door saying you turned up at the arranged time, hope all is well with them, please call for another appointment. It is worth considering that sometimes a genuine problem prevents a client from being there to have their hair done. Yes, they could have called, but sometimes people simply forget. Your clients are human, like you. Give them one more chance, then drop them if they prove unreliable twice.

Constant complainers
There are some clients who are simply never happy, and these will always be more of a drain on your time and resources than others. Only you can decide if the time and effort you are putting into a particular client is worth it. If you feel that a certain client is taking you away from other, more profitable, ventures, then it would be worth considering refusing to do their hair anymore. Give them a good few chances before dropping them, though, and make sure it really is that they are impossible to please – and not just that YOU can't please them!

Can never answer your phone
If you are finding it impossible to keep up with all the messages when you get home because you can't answer your phone in the day, try asking your clients to always book ahead. If the majority of your appointments are booked when you are actually with a client, the only phone calls you will receive will be from new clients, or people who need to

change their appointments. If clients are complaining they can't get hold of you, offer them a fixed time when you will always be able to answer the phone. It need only be a half-hour window, in the morning for example, or at lunch time. Choose a time when you will always be able to get to the phone, and then ask your clients to call then.

CHAPTER FIVE
FINANCIAL MATTERS

Now you are a business owner there are many financial considerations which you will need to take into a account and keep track of along the way. From Tax and VAT, to your cash book and banking, financial matters can seem never-ending to the self-employed. This section deals with all things financial, and aims to help you find your way through the mine field without too much difficulty.

KEEPING RECORDS

When you are running your own mobile hairdressing business, keeping records becomes a fact of life. There is no getting away from it – so don't try. This section will cover all the information that you need to keep track of, and give you advice on how to make sure your record keeping doesn't become too much of a chore!

Why keep records?

Not only is it a requirement of the Inland Revenue that all business owners keep records of their sales and expenses (the current guidelines are that you keep all records for six years), it is also an efficient way to do business. If you record everything you earn, and everything you spend, you will be able to tell where your money is going, and know if your business is growing or shrinking.

Financial records give you an overall picture, as well as a detailed one. If at some point in the future you need to cut costs, you will know what constitutes your biggest expense by looking at your records.

If you ever want to expand, perhaps into another town, or even by opening a salon, the records you have kept of your business's finances will be a useful tool in projecting your profits, for taking to a bank or other financial institution to gain backing.

And sometimes it is just nice to see how you're doing. Figures written down in black and white can be comforting. (Not so comforting if they are in the red!) To see a picture of how your business is growing from one year to the next is both empowering and encouraging.

What to record and how

On the most basic level, you need to record your sales (the money you charge clients) and your expenses (the money you spend on fuel, products, equipment etc). You can record this in a notebook if you want to. Keep all your receipts – ALL your receipts – in a shoebox, and then hand the whole lot over to your accountant at the end of the financial year.

TIP: *The financial year is the one the government says it is, not a year from when you started trading. Currently this is the*

*first week in April. If it will make things easier for you, begin
your business at this time also.*

If you choose to run your finances this way, your business
won't suffer and all will be well. But why pay out money to an
accountant when you could so easily do it yourself? Even if
you use an accountant's services for your year-end accounts
(instead of going down the self-assessment route – more
on this later), keeping your own records in an orderly and
methodical way will save you at least £200 - £300 a year.

The following section will take you through a basic accounting system, with samples of spreadsheets and layouts along
the way. Adapt them to meet the needs of your own business.

THE CASH BOOK

Daily or weekly cash in and out
Your cash book is your bible – everything that matters will
be recorded in here. It doesn't have to be an actual book –
a simple spreadsheet on your computer is probably better,
as many of the sums will be done for you. If you don't know
how to use Microsoft Excel yet, ask around for someone
who does and get them to teach you. It won't take long – you
don't need to know all of its fantastic features. Just how to
fill in the boxes and set up simple sums.

If your business is very busy, you may want to consider
keeping a record of your sales and expenses daily. If you
have a float (a sum of ready cash to give out as change and
to spend on such small things as parking), it will help you to
keep your accounts balanced. Keeping a daily record is very
quick and easy – simply sit down each evening and copy
out your sales from the information in your diary, and then
write down your expenditure from the receipts in your wallet
or purse.

TIP: *Get into the habit of asking for a receipt for EVERY-THING. If you aren't sure if you can claim tax relief for something, get a receipt for it anyway, just in case you can. At the end of each week, staple your receipts together and write the date and week number (with week 1 being the first week in April) on the top receipt.*

If you plan to keep a daily record, it may help to have all the days of the week on one sheet. This way it will be easy for you to 'cash up' at the end of each day and again at the end of each week. If you prefer to work longhand with your accounts, print off a record sheet like the following and fill it out as you go.

Date:		Float: £		Date:		Float: £		Date:		Float: £	
Service	Cash	Cheque	Retail	Service	Cash	Cheque	Retail	Service	Cash	Cheque	Retail
TOTALS	£	£	£	TOTALS	£	£	£	TOTALS	£	£	£
Cash +Float	£	cash exp.	£	Cash +Float	£	cash exp.	£	Cash +Float	£	cash exp.	£
Minus Exp.	£	Float over	£	Minus Exp.	£	Float over	£	Minus Exp.	£	Float over	£
Cash box	£	Run total	£	Cash box	£	Run total	£	Cash box	£	Run total	£
TOTAL SALES	£	HOURS		TOTAL SALES	£	HOURS		TOTAL SALES	£	HOURS	
Date:		Float: £		Date:		Float: £		Date:		Float: £	
Service	Cash	Cheque	Retail	Service	Cash	Cheque	Retail	Service	Cash	Cheque	Retail
TOTALS	£	£	£	TOTALS	£	£	£	TOTALS	£	£	£
Cash +Float	£	cash exp.	£	Cash +Float	£	cash exp.	£	Cash +Float	£	cash exp.	£
Minus Exp.	£	Float over	£	Minus Exp.	£	Float over	£	Minus Exp.	£	Float over	£
Cash box	£	Run total	£	Cash box	£	Run total	£	Cash box	£	Run total	£
TOTAL SALES	£	HOURS		TOTAL SALES	£	HOURS		TOTAL SALES	£	HOURS	

Let's go through each section of the cash sheet in detail, by looking at the completed example below:

DATE	15/03/2008	FLOAT	£
Service	Cash	Cheque	Retail
CBD	20		
Hi-lights	50		
CBD	20		
Wet Cut	15		
BD	15	55	
Hi-Lights		5	5
Shampoo			
TOTALS	£120	£60	£5
Cash+Float	£135	Cash exp.	£2.00
Minus Exp.	£133	Float over	£13.00
Cash box	£0	Run total	£180
TOTAL SALES	£180	HOURS	8

First of all, the date and the float are filled in. The float, as stated before, is an amount of cash you carry that is purely for the business. It is best to keep business money separate from your own, or things will get confusing. The float is currently £15.00.

Today, the hairdresser has seen six clients. She has written down the services and the prices in the appropriate columns. The first five paid cash, which is easy to record and keep track of. The float was used for change. The last client had Hi-lights and bought some shampoo, paying our hairdresser

by cheque. This is noted in the cheque column, with an extra entry in the Retail column so she can keep track of her retail sales separately.

Next, we tally up the cash sales and the cheque sales columns, and add these together in the Total Sales box (£180). Expenses which were paid for with cash from the float are also recorded on this sheet, in the Cash Exp box (£2.00). Our hairdresser checks the amount of cash in her money belt – she has £135 in total. This is exactly right: £120 cash sales plus £13 remaining from the float. The £13 is allocated for tomorrow's float. If more were needed this would be entered in the Cash box and deducted from the overall cash total for the day.

Finally, the running total box is completed – only £180 at the moment as this is the first day of the week, but this will be added to as the days go on – and then the number of hours worked is noted. This is worthwhile; at the end of each week you will be able to calculate your average hourly rate – and make sure it matches the minimum hourly charge you decided upon when you did your planning!

> **Consider this:** If all this seems a little like hard work, don't worry. This is a fairly complex example of the kind of figures a business needs to record on a daily basis. Yours may not need to be so thorough. However, complex though it may be, each set of figures is important. If you don't keep a track of your cheque payments you may become confused when you do your banking. If you don't have a float, you will end up using your own cash for change. Yes, it is all your own cash in theory, but you are far better off keeping the two separate.

Develop your own system of keeping records and then stick

to it. Summarise at the end of every week and let nothing slip through your fingers. Keep your records – your cash book and your receipts – safe and secure. If the tax man ever wants to see them, he has six years to go back and check up on you.

What you can claim tax as a taxable expense?
So what can you claim tax relief for and what isn't allowed? A taxable expense is basically anything that you buy that is directly needed for your business. This doesn't include your lunches, or that top you just had to buy because you look so good in it. (It can include a reasonable amount spent on clothing as you are entitled to buy a uniform for work.)

The following is not an exhaustive list. The Inland Revenue can advise you on the specifics of your own situation – and they are very helpful so don't be afraid to ask. As a basic guide you can offset reasonable amounts spent on:

- Fuel (keep receipts!)

- Car repairs (because your car is integral to your work, a reasonable amount on maintenance is allowed)

- All usable stock, such as peroxide, tints, perm solutions – anything you have bought to use on your clients' hair

- The products you have bought to sell to your clients

- Stationary – business cards, headed paper, information leaflets

- Advertising

- Any other marketing costs

- Electricity and heating for the part of your house you use to do your accounts (keep this reasonable, don't put forward the whole bill!)

- Clothing

- Equipment

- Costs of repairing and replacing equipment

- Bank charges

- Accountant services (if you decide to use one)

- Anything else that is directly necessary for your business and that is a sanctioned expense

If in any doubt at all, keep the receipt, make a note of the expenditure, and check with your accountant or your local tax office.

BANKING

As a self-employed mobile hairdresser you will need to have a business bank account. You will be unable to use your own personal current account, as most banks have a limit on the amount of cheques you can pay in per month. A business bank account will allow you to have cheques made out to your business name, rather than your own name (although you will obviously be able to pay in cheques made out to you as well).

Many banks offer business accounts with low charges, and some have charges suspended for an introductory period. Your banking charges shouldn't be too high for what you will be using the bank for (there will be no merchant banking fee, for example, unless you are accepting payments via credit card).

With your business account you will receive a paying-in book, a cheque book for paying suppliers or making other business-related payments, and possibly a credit or debit

card, depending on the type of account you have. Your bank may also sanction an overdraft facility for short-term borrowing.

TIP: *Most banks have a 'night-banking' facility – a secure deposit chute accessible from outside the bank at any time. This is extremely useful if you want to deposit your day's takings before going home, to avoid keeping large amounts of cash on you. Simply fill in a paying-in slip, put the cash and cheques into one of the bags supplied, and pop them in the chute.*

If you deal mainly in cash, you will want to bank your money at least every other day. If you have a lot of cheque transactions, however, once a week should be fine. Always be aware of your personal safety when carrying cash – and never risk it for money! Financial losses can be written off, but your health and wellbeing are priceless.

Another reason for getting your cash in the bank is that it can start earning interest. Shop around for banks for business accounts which pay interest, but if you can't find one, choose an account which is manageable online. This way you can transfer your balance to one of the many online web-saver accounts which usually pay a good rate of interest. Moving your money backwards and forwards like this is a little time-consuming, but is worthwhile – the interest you gain will at least offset the bank's charges.

SELF-ASSESSMENT AND TAX RETURNS

A few years ago the government introduced Self-Assessment – a simplified way of completing a tax return for the self-employed, or those with more than one taxable income. Once you register as self-employed (see *Chapter One:*

Getting Started) you will begin to receive Self-Assessment forms regularly from the Inland Revenue.

The government is often accused of using too much meaningless jargon, and whether this is true or not, the term Self-Assessment is certainly misleading – mainly because you don't actually have to fill out the form yourself. You can pay an accountant to do it for you, and many business people do just this as they find the forms confusing.

The Inland Revenue have, however, taken steps to make the forms pretty much fool-proof, and offer an online service where you can fill in your Self-Assessment form (and save it for later if you can't complete it all in one go), and then have it checked automatically before you submit it. The online service will even work out your tax liability (the amount of tax you will have to pay) before you submit.

If your figures are relatively straight forward – and many mobile hairdressing accounts are – you shouldn't have too much trouble filling in a Self-Assessment form online. Below are a few pointers to help you through the process:

• Have everything ready before you begin. Although you can save the form and go back later, if you have made the time in your busy schedule to get the blasted thing done you might as well finish it off! You will need your weekly or monthly cash book (or details of all your sales), all your receipts for the tax year (April to April, remember), your National Insurance number, details of any savings you have and whether you have paid tax on them, any information relating to any other work you have completed in the tax year, benefits you have collected, or any other income at all.

- Add up your total sales and expenses before you start. Your expenses cannot include your own personal survival budget or your living expenses – these are direct costs only. Putting forward most of your fuel is fine, as you use your car for your business all day, every day. But remember that that the fuel you use for personal use is not tax-deductable.

- If your total turnover (turnover means sales before you deduct your expenses – what is left is called profit) doesn't exceed a certain limit (currently £15,000), you can submit only three line accounts. This literally means three lines of information: your sales, your expenses, and your profit – the first figure minus the second. Hopefully, however, your sales will exceed this amount so your expenses will need to be broken down into various categories, such as fuel, goods for re-sale, equipment etc. See the Inland Revenue's website for further information.

- Don't be tempted to lie. As a self-employed person your personal allowance (the amount you can earn before you pay tax) will be generous and there are many, many things you are allowed to deduct from your sales before you reach the final figure (your pre-tax profits) you will pay any tax on at all. The Tax Man isn't stupid – they have seen it all before. They have models of all businesses of all sizes and if your accounts don't stack up with what they consider 'normal' for a mobile hairdressing business they will investigate you further. You don't want this. Be honest and fair, and you will get the same back.

- Keep a copy of your Self-Assessment form once you have completed it. At the end of the online process you have the opportunity to print a copy for your records. Do so – it will help you to fill out your tax return next year.

Paying your taxes – when and how?

One more important point to cover regarding tax, and that is making payment. As previously stated, payments are made retrospectively – but they are also made 'on account', meaning in advanced. Confused? You will be.

Once the Inland Revenue has your final Self-Assessment submission, your tax burden for the year will be calculated. (You can opt to work it out yourself or for them to work it out for you. Let them do it. If you get it wrong they will only make you pay it back, and if the Inland Revenue overcharge you they usually realise before you do anyway!) Payment of your tax is due by the January of the following year. But – the Inland Revenue also like for you to pay half of your expected taxes for the coming (or current) financial year.

Now, in the long run this is a good thing, and won't make a lot of difference. Next year you only need to pay the other half because you paid half last year. Plus half of the year to come, but then you'll only have half to pay next year – and on and on. The only time this can be difficult is at the end of your first year in business, because you will be liable to pay all of the previous year's tax plus half of next year's.

You can apply to have a reduction in the amount you need to pay on account, usually on the basis you expect your next year's profits to be lower than this year's. In the case of a growing business, however, this is unlikely to be the case. The best thing you can do is take the money out of the bank account you have been saving it in every month and pay the Tax Man like a good citizen.

What do you mean, you haven't been saving? You were aware that at some point in the future you would have to pay a little tax, weren't you? I'm sure it was mentioned right at the start of this book.

In order to pay your tax bill on time (penalties are charged for late payments and these are very, very steep), you will need to put by a sum of money every month. The basic tax rate is currently 25% of all earnings above your personal allowance. This varies from person to person, and circumstance to circumstance. As a rough guide, if you are putting away 20% of all you earn, every month, you should be able to pay your taxes without dipping into any other savings – possibly. This should not be taken as a cast-iron guarantee, however. Talk to an accountant or the Inland Revenue for expert advice.

National Insurance

National Insurance is an incredibly complicated subject, and not one that can be adequately covered here. There are four levels of NI at present, with different rules for certain trades, and many different levels depending on marital status and earnings.

As a self-employed person you will be liable to pay Class Four National Insurance at the same time as you pay your Income Tax. This will be calculated for you from your final figures. You can also pay Voluntary Class Two contributions which count towards your state pension and any benefits you might need to access in the future.

Once again, the jargon is misleading. Voluntary isn't really voluntary. You can apply not to pay, if your income is low or you have reason to believe you don't need to. Again, you will need current and expert advice on this topic, so speak to your local tax office. Class Two contributions won't break the bank, however, and are currently paid at £2.30 a week.

Staying On Top Of It All

You are pretty much an expert yourself at finances now. You have mastered spreadsheets, planning and forecasting,

break-even figures, and so much more. Now it is time to bring it all together and develop a system for keeping on top of your business.

ANALYSING YOUR SITUATION

It is easy to get so caught up in working 'in' the business, that you forget you also need to spend at least a little time working 'on' the business. Ask anyone who has been self-employed for any period of time and they will tell you that being good at your job and working hard is only half the battle.

You are no longer just a hairdresser. No, you're not. You are a hairdresser and an accountant, a business advisor, a secretary, a marketing executive, an advertising special-ist, a customer relations expert and, most importantly, a financial whizz!

All you need to do in order to make sure you are still heading in the right direction is spend a little time each month looking at your accounts. Ask yourself certain questions: Was last month better than the one before? Is my client list growing? What is my average hourly rate? Is it higher than this time last year? In other words, be curious about your business. Curiosity will keep you on top of everything that makes your business what it is, and will keep you fresh, always looking for ways to improve.

If you do find that your business is sliding in the wrong direc-tion, take any necessary steps immediately. Don't bury your head in the sand and hope it will all get better by itself. It won't. Go back to the section on building your business and begin to use all the methods at your disposal for gaining new clients and turning things around.

CHAPTER SIX

GROWING YOUR BUSINESS

Now you have a successful business, and you are probably working flat-out and earning a fantastic salary as a reward for all your efforts. Congratulations. You're nearly there. But not quite...

If you were hoping to hear that this is it, now, you have reached the top and success is guaranteed for life, you clearly haven't been listening too well. Remember the motto of all good businesses?

"If your business isn't growing it is shrinking."

That's right. Never forget this. It will always be the difference between you and the stories you hear about those high percentages of businesses who go under and close. As soon as you start to feel happy, to feel that you have finally arrived at a point where you can stop searching for new clients, or thinking of that next angle – worry. You are about to get stale. Give it another six months, a year if you are lucky, and work will begin to trail off, your client list will shrink, and you won't have the energy to figure out why.

Okay, maybe this sounds a little extreme. It is just such a terrible shame to see so many businesses fail when they started out with such promise. After putting in so much hard work in those early stages, why do business owners lose their enthusiasm and let things slip away?

This won't happen to you. Why? Because you have this book. You have at your fingertips all the tools you need to keep on growing, and growing, and growing...

And the next tool in your kit is where to take your business as you head into the future, and to meet all the challenges and opportunities head-on.

MAXING OUT

One of the downfalls of many a successful mobile hair-dresser is reaching a point where you physically cannot do any more work. Say you are already working a six day week (you must give yourself at least one day off, health and safety insist upon it). You start the day at eight a.m. with trims and blow-drys for your business clients. You stuff down a quick sandwich en route for lunch, and then work through until eight, nine, sometimes ten o'clock at night, every night of the week. Even Saturdays.

This is not a life, of course, but many hairdressers end up in this position – a victim of their own success. They can't take a holiday, their clients would go crazy. They mustn't get sick. Because they are so good and so dedicated, new clients are calling all the time, but not only is the hairdresser too busy to answer their phone – when would they fit in the new client?

This is a dangerous situation to be in. You need those new clients, for the reasons we have explored at length in this book. You must always be open to taking on fresh people.

So what are you to do if you become so successful you have completely 'maxed out'?

PUTTING PRICES UP

The first, and not always immediately obvious, thing to do is to put your prices up. This has a number of good effects:

Firstly, it increases your profits overnight. Even if you only add an extra £1.00 to each of your prices, if you are seeing 30 clients a week this is an extra £120 a month instantly. Without you doing any more work. Sound good? Read on.

The second, possible, effect is that the price increase slows down your business slightly. This will depend on how heavily you hike your prices, so you will have to think about the level of your increase very carefully. It may sound counterproductive to raise your prices in such a way as to reduce the number of clients you see in a week, but if you are completely maxed out with work this may be the only way to give yourself some breathing space without actually losing clients.

But, you say, what if I do lose clients? This is a possibility, especially if your price rise is significant. However, you have to ask yourself how valuable those clients were to you if they chose to go elsewhere rather than pay a little extra? (Again, it depends on the rise in prices.) Some mobile hairdressers use price rises as a way of deliberately losing unprofitable clients when they reach maximum capacity (when you can't take on any new clients because you simply don't have time). This is a sensible strategy, and often a very successful one.

Regular Price Increases

Often, a hairdresser maxes out because he has failed to increase his prices for a long period of time. It is good practice to put your prices up once a year (no more), by at

least £1.00. This way, your clients are accustomed to it and understand that it is your way of meeting the needs of your own increasing costs, due to inflation and natural rises in the costs of living.

If clients complain, you can ask them: 'Do you ever get a pay rise at work?' They will no doubt answer that they do. Then you can explain that, as you are your own boss, you don't have anybody to give you a pay rise, you have to make it happen yourself. And this is how it happens. Most clients will be happy to pay the extra – providing it is only one or two pounds.

If you increase your prices for the reasons stated above, and increase them significantly to meet the current market level because you've failed to do so for a while, many of your clients will be understandably confused, and possibly upset. Below we will look at how to handle price increases sensitively, but consider this – if your successful clientele is built upon having clients who won't pay the going rate for their hair, then how successful is it?

Better to have fewer clients, who are happy to pay what you are worth, and leave a few gaps for new clients to fill, than to work flat out for next to nothing!

How to deal with a price increase sensitively

When you increase your prices it is important to let your clients know ahead of time. This means they must know before you ask them for the extra money. There are two ways of doing this:

1. Send all your clients a letter telling them about the price increase. Set out your new prices and say the date from which they will take effect. This should be far enough into the future for your clients to be able to

cancel their appointment if they choose not to pay the extra – you don't want this, but it is their right to do so should they wish.

2. For a period of about six weeks, tell all your clients that next time you see them the price of their hair cut will be going up. Be clear about how much and don't be apologetic. If they ask why, give them the reasons detailed above – rises in the cost of living, fuel, insurance, the products you buy to use on their hair – everything increases all of the time. It is called an economy. As soon as you are sure you have seen all of your clients, start to charge the new prices.

You may find the first method the best, as it is cleaner and more straight forward. You turn up after the specified date, do your client's hair, then ask for the new payment. If your client looks confused, you can remind her of your letter. Remember to carry plenty of change – if you are putting up your price of £20 to £21, it will not be so easy for your client to merely give you a twenty pound note!

If there are a group of clients who you feel would be adversely affected by your increase, but you still want to put up your prices for the reasons above, why not offer a discount to them? Maybe you have a couple of pensioners in your round and you feel bad about charging them more – especially if they don't take up a lot of your time (you are allowed to be human when you are a business person).

There is nothing to stop you offering individual discounts for any reason you choose: loyalty, age, place of work, referring lots of clients – the list is endless. Just make sure you don't end up offering so many discounts your price increase becomes meaningless

Working out a reasonable increase

If you are increasing your prices due to maxing out, the amount of your increase will depend on whether you have been regularly increasing your prices in line with inflation every year. If you have, then simply add a reasonable amount onto each of your prices; a £1.00 to £3.00 increase across the board should be sufficient to have an effect.

If you haven't increased your prices for a long time – or, indeed, since you set up the business – a certain amount of market research will be needed first. Go back to the section of this book on Planning, and remind yourself of the ins and outs of market research – particularly researching the competition. Armed with the information relating to the current competition in your area (mobile and salon hairdressers), compare their prices to yours.

If you haven't increased your prices for a while you will probably find a discrepancy between your prices and those of the competition. Consider your experience, the size of your client base, and the type of clients you mainly see, and set your new prices accordingly. If you are top-end, match closely to the best salon you surveyed. If you are a little more middle-of-the-road, pitch yourself in the middle of the mobile hairdressers and the salons. And so on. Pricing is not the time to be either modest or arrogant – you must be honest with yourself about where you are placed in the current market.

Remember to take your costs into account. Go back through the budgeting exercise you did when you first started your business – your survival budget will almost certainly have changed, and your sales may no longer meet your needs. Work out your minimum hourly cost. Is this reflected in your prices? If you have been trading for a few years and have a healthy clientele, your hourly rate should be far in excess of your minimum.

YOUR 'A' CLIENTS

Strategies to consider if you are in a 'maxed-out' situation include looking at dropping – or at least relegating – clients which aren't as profitable as others. This isn't an exercise for the faint-hearted – but if you are that faint-hearted you won't last long in business anyway.

If you are running all over town dishing out wet cuts and cheap trims to clients who drain you of energy and time, you will know exactly what we are talking about here. If you have a handful of enriching, energising clients who care about their hair and are willing to spend money on it, you may well wish you could clone them. You will probably wish you could spend more time in their company than the company of those clients who make you look forward to leaving rather than arriving!

The good news is – you can. You can attract more and more of the type of clients you love to see, the kind who make your day feel worthwhile and who you are genuinely sad to say goodbye to. These are your 'A' clients, and to make your business even more of a success you must focus your energies on these clients alone.

This means not only focussing your efforts on attracting them, through the right kind of advertising and marketing (referrals from existing 'A' clients are a great way to do this), you must also focus on keeping happy the ones you've got, and making room for more.

How to identify an 'A' client

First of all, sit down now with your diary and a pen and paper, and identify your 'A' clients. They are the ones who spend the most money with you, for one thing. They are the clients you see regularly, who never mess you about, and who are

always happy and realistic about their hair. They either have enough money to spend on their hair, or they prioritise their hair very highly.

Your 'A' clients have regular cuts and colours, are happy to try something new occasionally, they may use the shampoos and conditioners you sell, and they have loads of friends they could recommend you to (often because they are genuinely nice people).

However, these may also be the clients you forget about most of the time, as they are the ones who cause you the least amount of trouble – these are the ones you are in danger of taking for granted.

Putting them first
Stop! Make a list of these clients and pin it to the front of your diary. From now on you will treat these clients like royalty. You will never be late, or rushed, or preoccupied when you see them. You will listen even more carefully than usual. You will excel yourself whenever you go anywhere near their hair.

Your 'A' clients are the backbone of your business. Collectively they are probably bringing in about 80% of your revenue – but you may only be giving them 20% of your attention. This is because other, more time consuming clients, take up your attention – for all the wrong reasons. Your 'A' clients won't know they are 'A' clients. (If a client acts like you should drop everything for them and believes they are more important than anyone else they are definitely NOT an 'A' client!)

The second thing you must do is make room for more and more 'A' clients. How? By ensuring you aren't too busy attending to your 'B' and 'C' clients, that's how!

MORE MONEY – LESS EFFORT

Once you have put the above into place, are working on your 'A' list and charging the right prices, what else can you do to improve your business? The answer lies in mastering the art of working smart not hard.

Maximising each visit

Now you have to up your game and look for ways to make the most out of each visit. With your 'A' clients, this should be easy. If you turn up to do a haircut, talk to your client about colour. If you are there to colour their hair, talk about products. If your client has a colour and already uses your products, talk about hair-additions.

You get the picture. The idea here is to 'up-sell' each client as much as possible. This is a practice used in retail all the time – when was the last time you bought anything electrical without being offered insurance, an extended guarantee or a service warranty? Shoe shops try to sell you leather guard. Even McDonalds ask you to 'make it large'.

Another way to maximise each visit is to try and lump together as many of your clients as possible in one place. (This is only possible if they know each other, of course, but should be easy once more and more clients come from referrals.) Not only does this save on fuel costs and time, it also creates a competitive atmosphere – if one of your client's is buying your shampoo, another will want to try it too.

Selling hairdressing products

If you aren't already selling products to your clients, now is the time to start. You won't be able to capitalize on your 'A' clients without them. These clients are looking for a one-stop-shop – they truly want you to provide everything for them. They have great hair, thanks to you. They want their

hair to look good all the time. They want to know they are using the right thing. And they look to you, their hairdresser, to tell them what that is. Don't let them down.

Choose a range you are comfortable with – and one that is likely to be around for a long time. Don't be tempted by special offers at the wholesaler for product ranges which may not be there the next time you visit. And remember, the products must be ones your clients can't buy at the local chemist or supermarket.

Don't set your prices too high. There is no need to have a huge mark-up on the products you sell – they have a higher value than merely monetary. If your clients love the shampoo you sell them, and can only get it from you, they are more likely to call you back again. And if they run out in between haircuts, they will have to call you and book a haircut just to get their shampoo!

Always supply your products in a nice bag with a few business cards. Touches like this mark you out as a professional. Never underestimate the power of those little touches.

Including the whole family

Another way of maximising each of your visits to clients is to make sure you are seeing to the hair of every member of the family. Yes, even babies need haircuts! And husbands, teenagers, grandmas and grandads... There is no reason why you shouldn't be cutting each family member's hair whenever you visit. Again, this saves costs for you, and opens up a whole new market of products and services, such as:

- Teenagers will love hair-additions in bright, funky colours. They will also tell all their friends where they got it.

- Guys are getting wise to products, and enjoy having the latest waxes and gels to make their hair look great.

- Win over grandma and then persuade her to have a little colour next time you visit – it will knock years off her!

RENTING A CHAIR

Now for a few ideas for those hairdressers who are looking for something a little different; who are looking to expand or move into other areas. The first of these is renting a chair in a salon.

If you rent a chair you are still self-employed – which means you are still liable for your own taxes and national insurance, even though you are working in a salon. How it usually works is, the salon charges you a rent for the space, or chair, that you use, and you keep everything else you make after that has been paid. There is often a charge for stock, unless you have a complicated arrangement where you provide your own. You may also be asked to contribute to the wages of any apprentices and the receptionist.

Let's look at some of the pros and cons:

PRO: You are in one place and your clients come to you. If you are getting a little fed up of travelling around this could be very attractive.

CON: Whatever you save in fuel and car repairs, you will spend in your rent.

PRO: Hairdressing is a lot more comfortable in a salon, with an adjustable chair, backwashes and a proper mirror in front of you. All the plug sockets will be in the right place, your equipment will be all around you, and it is so much easier to make clients look great in a salon environment.

CON: In order to be in line with the salon's prices you will probably have to hike yours up, unless you are already

positioning yourself in line with top salons in your area. You may lose some clients if you do this – and you may be relying on your existing clients to make the move to renting a chair work financially.

PRO: You'll have colleagues to talk to and share stories with.

CON: Although you will be self-employed, you will probably still feel as though the salon manager is your boss – kind of. Only you know how you will handle this.

PRO: You will be able to see far more clients in your day because you won't be travelling around.

CON: The pace of your work will be far more frantic. No more cups of tea with a client while her colour develops!

WORKING WITH OTHERS

Maybe you need to expand a little but don't fancy renting a chair in a salon. You could consider taking on help – otherwise known as staff.

This is fairly problematic for a mobile hairdresser, but not impossible. When it works, it is usually when two people who trust each other work together. You would need to think of whoever you work with as more of a partner than an employee. Sharing your clients is not a decision to be taken lightly. But if it will help you to grow and expand, it could make all the difference.

One idea would be for your clients to pay you directly, and then for you to pay your colleague. Bear in mind, however, that you would then be an employer and would be liable for all the responsibilities that comes with it. Another option is to operate in a similar way to rent a chair; to hand over some of your clients for your colleague to take care of and have them

pay you a monthly fee for this. Yet another is for you to take a percentage of everything your colleague does.

Whichever option you go for, it will be worth getting some kind of agreement drawn up with a solicitor. Working relationships can go badly wrong, even if you were friends before. Especially if you were friends before!

EXPANDING INTO OTHER AREAS

The last idea we will look into is expanding into other areas, such as nail extensions, manicures and beauty. If you are getting a little stale or bored with hairdressing, but have a successful business and a large clientele, you already have the structure to add lots of other services your clients might be interested in. At the very least, you will be increasing your skills base and having fun along the way.

Nails, beauty and more

Nail technicians are the new beauty therapists. Whether it is down to the rise of the WAG, or just women taking more of a pride in their hands, but nails are becoming an increasingly important part of a woman's beauty package – and fortunes are being spent on them every day!

From simple manicures – French, of course – to nail extensions, good nail technicians are in demand. Like hairdressing, nail extensions and manicures are great for repeat business, don't need too much equipment (you can buy portable nail-bars and fold-up stools to carry around to people's houses with you), and the business is highly profitable.

As a hairdresser, the chances are you already have a high level of the creativity and dexterity to make a good nail technician. There are many courses which offer varying degrees of qualifications – some more useful than others. If you are

considering adding nails to your repertoire of skills, find the best course you can afford and invest in yourself. This will give you the confidence to market yourself properly – and not seem like nothing more than a hairdresser who is now doing nails!

TIP: *If you are confused about which course to take, call the best nail-bar in your area and ask them which qualifications they insist their staff have. Take whichever course they say.*

Beauty is a slightly more complicated venture. For one thing, the skills require a far longer period of time to train for, and due to the procedures carried out by beauticians these days, the standards of the training are very high – it is not something you could reasonably learn in a few weeks.

Moving into this area should only be considered as a complete career change. Of course, nothing is stopping you from combining the two skills once you are qualified in both, but that is the key – you need to be qualified in both. Time out from your hairdressing would be needed in order to take a career in beauty seriously, during which time you would no doubt lose your hairdressing clients. If this is the route for you, once again you should get advice about which course to take.

An 'in-between' option is to add a few beauty-type treatments to your hairdressing services. You could quite happily offer eye-lash tinting to your existing clients, along with make-up. You could even sell a range of make-up and beauty products.

Whichever route you take to increase your business, always give it your best shot and as much enthusiasm as you can. But always remember you were a hairdresser first, and will probably always come back to this in the end.

Have fun with your business, and keep it fresh. That way it will nurture you and provide you with a wonderful lifestyle for years and years to come.

Happy hairdressing!

FURTHER RESOURCES

Organisations
Freelance Hair And Beauty Federation www.fhbf.org.uk
Professional membership organisation for freelance hairdressers and beauty therapists.

Useful Websites
Balmain www.balmainhair.com
Hair extensions and additions, training available.

Inland Revenue www.hmrc.gov.uk
For all tax related information and support.

Salons Direct www.salonsdirect.co.uk
Large wholesaler with outlets across the country.

Sally Hair and Beauty www.sallybeauty.com
Wholesaler, also open to the public, runs courses at selected branches.

FreeIndex www.freeindex.co.uk
A directory of mobile hairdressers (along with other services) which features high up on search engine rankings.

Home Hairdresser UK www.homehairdresser.co.uk
A directory specifically for mobile hairdressers, also offering web design and hosting service. Good Google rankings.